NEW SAT ESSAY

HARVARD STUDENTS' ESSAY ANALYSIS

SAT ◆ ACT ◆ IELTS ◆ TOEFL

SAT HACKERS

By San

About the book & author

Whether you are preparing for SAT, ACT, IELTS, or TOEFL, all the tests can fall into one category: College Level Standardized Test. In that sense, the scoring rubrics of all the standardized tests are very similar to each other. The tests (SAT, ACT, IELTS, TOEFL, SSAT, or K 8~12 in class essay) you are preparing will measure the following three major sub-categories:

Reading: How thoroughly you understand a reading passage or a question (prompt) by asking what is the central point of the argument based on the evidence you found.

Analysis: Analysis measures your logic, stylistic and persuasive devices that you can commend.

Writing: Writing should be holistic in its organization with precise sentence structure, flawless syntax, style, and tone.

Here, in this book, students can find how Harvard students write their essays and follow their reasoning analytically with almost free of error.

San, for over 20 years of his career, worked in various educational industries.
From college entrance consulting to teaching standardized tests such as SAT / ACT / IELTS / TOEFL / LSAT/ GRE, he has been helping numerous students to enter their top choice universities.
San is currently living in North Vancouver, B.C. Canada, where he teaches and write books to further students' needs and realize their ambitions.

For enrollment through skype lesson, please contact to the author using his email: satvancouver@gmail.com

Dedicated to my wife, Eun Jun and my dog, Okong

CONTENTS

CONTENTS

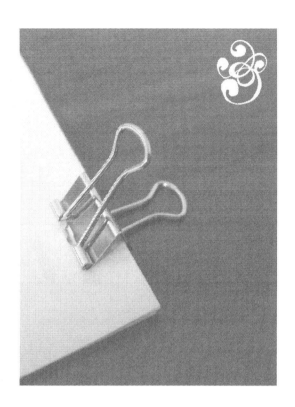

Chapter 1

**Understanding How
Scores Are Measured
&
The Elements in Your Essay**

Understanding How Scores are Measured

As mentioned on the previous introductory page, all the standardized tests measure students' analytical skills, writing skills, and the passage understanding skills. In order to earn the highest possible scores, we need to understand how students' scores are measured. For the score rubric guidelines in this book, I have used SAT Essay scoring analysis, which is definitely applicable not only to SAT but also to any other standardized tests.

The Essay Prompt

First, let's discuss about the prompt or question.
- You will be asked to find evidence like facts, supporting claims, or data from the passage.
- You will be asked to find how the author develops his/her ideas to connect claims based on reasoning
- You will be asked to find stylistic or persuasive devices such as vocabulary choice, emotional appeal.

Based on your findings, you should write an essay to explain how the writer (Reading passage or Question) creates his/her argument to the audience. On your essay should you have facts and features listed above.

Your SAT Essay Score

Your SAT Essay score will be measured by the two people who will reward you between 1 and 4 points in each of three sections: Reading, Analysis, and Writing.

Reading: You should understand the central ideas of the reading and bring this idea with the evidence found from the reading.

Analysis: Analysis should include logic, stylistic and persuasive devices the author employees.

Writing: Writing should be holistic in its organization with precise sentence structure, flawless syntax, style, and tone.

Scoring Rubric

Reading Scoring Guide
♦ Demonstrates thorough comprehension of the source text.
♦ Shows an understanding of the text's central idea(s) and of most important details and how they interrelate, demonstrating a comprehensive understanding of the text.
♦ Is free of errors of fact or interpretation with regard to the text.
♦ Makes skillful use of textual evidence (quotations, paraphrases, or both), demonstrating a complete understanding of the source text.

Analysis Scoring Guide
♦ Offers an insightful analysis of the source text and demonstrates a sophisticated understanding of the analytical task.
♦ Offers a thorough, well-considered evaluation of the author's use of evidence, reasoning, and/or stylistic and persuasive elements, and/or feature(s) of the student's own choosing.
♦ Contains relevant, sufficient, and strategically chosen support for claim(s) or point(s) made.
♦ Focuses consistently on those features of the text that are most relevant to addressing the task.

Writing Scoring Guide
♦ Is cohesive and demonstrates a highly effective use and command of language.
♦ Includes a precise central claim.
♦ Includes a skillful introduction and conclusion. The response demonstrates a deliberate and highly effective progression of ideas both within paragraphs and throughout the essay.
♦ Has a wide variety in sentence structures. The response demonstrates a consistent use of precise word choice. The response maintains a formal style and objective tone.
♦ Shows a strong command of the conventions of standard written English and is free or virtually free of errors.

The Elements in Each Paragraph of Your Essay

The most pivotal guideline in the reading scoring is to find whether student's essay demonstrates thorough comprehension of the source text, and shows an understanding of the text's central idea.

Central Argument (Clear Thesis)

To start with, each of the paragraphs on your essay, including introduction, body paragraphs, and conclusion, should contain a clear thesis (argument), to where the reader easily can identify his thesis—normally the topic sentence on each paragraph.

Argument

Argument does not mean quarrel, complain, or disagree.

Argument is Reason + conclusion.
Reasons are synonymous with: premises, evidence, data, propositions, proofs, and verification. Conclusions are synonymous with: claims, actions, verdicts, and opinions.

Argument example :

Don't trust John	because	John is a politician
Conclusion	*indicator*	*Reason*

The above example implies the assumption that all politicians can't not be trusted.

Ask yourself if the assumption is qualified to be an argument by either the statement is:
1. known to be true
2. is reasonable to accept without further arguments.

since, while, because, for, for the reason that, as are "Reason indicators".
- *therefore, thus, so, hence, it follows that are indicators to yield conclusion statement.*

sometimes there will be no indicator at all when sentence itself is intended as a reason, a conclusion.

Facts vs. Theory vs. Opinion vs. Faith

- Facts can be proven
- Theory is to be proven but should not be confused with fact
- Opinions may or may not be based on sound reasoning
- Faith is not subject to proof by its nature

Supporting Details

As written on the Reading Score Rubric, you should make skillful use of textual evidence (quotations, paraphrases, or both), demonstrating a complete understanding of the source text.

Analysis of the Central Argument & Supporting Details

Followed by the supporting details, you should write analysis that is identified on the Analysis and Writing rubric. Analysis can be made through the following processes:

thorough, well-considered evaluation of the author's use of evidence

Analysis scoring guide indicates that your essay must present evidence from the passage and make it through, well-considered evaluation.

Support Your Points With Concrete Evidence From the Passage

-Specific data and facts

Specific data and facts will normally be found on your Reading passage.

Example of Specific Data and Facts Evidence with numerical text:

> For instance, the University of California at Los Angeles received upwards of 50,000 applications last year. Standardized tests might be a terrible system, but they are better than the alternatives.

Example of Specific Data and Facts Evidence Without Numerical Text:

♦ The good news is that debate about the importance of standardized testing in college admissions finally seems to be spreading to those with the power to reform the system. Indeed, at the National Association for College Admissions Counseling (NACAC) Conference held last week, discussion about the importance of standardized testing took the limelight. And NACAC is taking action—it formed a Commission on the Use of Standardized Tests in Undergraduate Admission, chaired by Harvard Dean of Admissions William R. Fitzsimmons '67, which will issue a report next year.

♦ For instance, the University of California at Los Angeles received upwards of 50,000 applications last year. Standardized tests might be a terrible system, but they are better than the alternatives.

Anecdotal Evidence Example

Just when I was starting to get used to the passionate debates that characterize meals in Annenberg, a recent dinner conversation threw me a curveball. Last week, I had the unique—and frustrating—privilege of dining with the last individual on earth who does not believe in global warming.

Thorough, well-considered evaluation of the author's use of reasoning

Analysis scoring guide indicates that essay must present the author's use of reasoning and make it through, well-considered evaluation.

Reasoning

In the SAT essay reading passage, you must find more than one reasoning statements and conclusion statements. In fact, reasoning appears in several complicated forms.

Counterargument

Counterargument can normally be found in the introductory paragraph. In order to intensify argument, writer employs opposite opinion that the writer disagree with or commonly misunderstood-concept briefly followed by contradictory conjunction such as "however", "but", "although", "despite the fact that", "while", etc.

Example with Counterargument

Privacy in our society is clearly diminishing: We carry devices everywhere we go so that people can reach us, the credit cards we use let any corporation view our purchases, and the Internet has allowed an unprecedented level of information to be publicly available. While this trend can be troubling, simple-minded reactions are not warranted.

Stylistic and Persuasive Elements

Stylistic and Persuasive elements seasons your reasoning fantastically.

Some of the examples of stylistic and persuasive elements found in passage are Irony, Paradox, Juxtaposition, Similes, Metaphors, and Adjectives.

Reading passage contains various forms of reasoning devices such as irony / paradox / juxtaposition / counterargument

Irony

A Irony is a rhetorical device, literary technique, or event in which what appears, on the surface, to be the case, differs radically from what is actually the case. Irony usually contains humorous tone in essence.

Example of Irony

Despite her frantic claims that she was "kidding that she planted bombs at the airport," Dutch officials showed up at the Rotterdam native's house and arrested her on the spot, drawing to a close a news story that would have been completely fruitless had it not provided me a topic to write about. For that, you and I both have @QueenDemetriax_'s unreliable frontal lobe to thank.

Paradox

A paradox is a statement that, despite apparently sound reasoning from true premises, leads to a self-contradictory or a logically unacceptable conclusion. Some logical **paradoxes** are known to be invalid arguments but are still valuable in promoting critical thinking.

Paradox Example

We've been taught since childhood to spend when we know we'll have more and save precisely when we have little. Though this seems fairly reasonable, it certainly doesn't sound right to teach farmers to gorge themselves during good harvests and only attempt to store grain in bad harvests.

Juxtaposition

Juxtaposition is a literary technique in which two seemingly opposing ideas, places, characters or their actions are placed side by side in a narrative. Juxtaposition usually contains positive and negative values such as poor vs. rich, evil vs. God.

Juxtaposition Example

How can you reconcile social media's giddy artificiality with death's stone-cold reality? How can you connect a corpse to a profile picture?

By displaying nothing more than instances of frivolity, by encouraging users to disguise themselves inside a sunny-beach persona, social media prevents the acknowledgement of deeper emotions, such as grief.

Against a background of party photos and emojis, mortality loses all of its defining gravitas. The deceased become abject and even absurd—they simply can't coexist with this sepia-tinted world in which every comment is an inside joke.

Put it this way: There is nothing more unsettling than the Facebook profile of a dead teenager.

I think the uneasy feeling derives from the lightheartedness of the content that dominates any social media platform. There are airy "lol" comments; there are witty photo captions.

*giddy: dizzy

Introduction paragraph Example

Last October, LVMH allocated $143 million to found a private museum of contemporary art for its Louis Vuitton Foundation, and commissioned architect Frank Gehry to design and construct it in Paris's Bois de Boulogne. Even for the multinational conglomerate that runs Louis Vuitton, Moët, Hennessy, and 66 other luxury goods companies—all of which you've definitely heard of—this is a considerable investment worth investigating. What merits a price tag of $143 million? In part, social capital. When prompted to explain why he wished to open the Louis Vuitton Foundation, Bernard Arnault, the CEO of LVMH,said, "We wanted to present Paris with an extraordinary space for art and culture, and demonstrate daring and emotion by entrusting Frank Gehry with the construction of an iconic building for the 21st century." Indeed, Arnault was able to successfully build his museum on a plot of land that had previously been denied to several other land developers. While these competitors wished to construct office buildings and business centers, Arnault was granted control of the land because his proposition was deemed to be a noble endeavor to create a public work.

But in a city that already boasts high concentrations of both art and culture, this was an ambitious—maybe even superfluous—undertaking.

It is clear to me that the goal of creating a rich, new ground for cultural discovery was only of secondary importance to Arnault. Though the museum has staged several provoking shows recently, in its opening weeks it showed nothing more than a condensed version of Arnault's private collection.

Appeal to the Reader Emotion

From the SAT essay reading passage you can find often appeal to the emotion elements. Appeal to the emotion is the direct antithesis to reasoning, lacking logical approach. These are usually carried out by author's tone, rhetorical questions, or personal anecdote.

Example of a Personal Anecdote

When I was starting to get used to the passionate debates that characterize meals in Annenberg, a recent dinner conversation threw me a curveball. Last week, I had the unique—and frustrating—privilege of dining with the last individual on earth who does not believe in global warming.

Example of Rhetorical Question

Meanwhile, Western nations were recently involved in rewriting the Iraqi and Afghani constitutions, both of which prominently enshrined the position of Islam. Does this analysis affirm the warning that "the elevation of Iranian-style theocrats," as one critical academic put it at the time, would undo the democratic order?

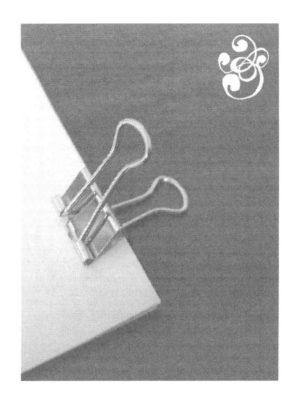

Chapter 2

Essay Analysis

SAMPLE ESSAY 1

Essay Prompt

As you read the passage below, consider how Idrees M. Kahloon uses

♦ evidence, such as facts or examples, to support claims.

♦ reasoning to develop ideas and to connect claims and evidence.

♦ stylistic or persuasive elements, such as word choice or appeals to emotion, to add power to the ideas expressed.

Adopted from Idrees M. Kahloon "Are democracy and constitutional Islam at odds?"
© January 29, 2016 The Crimson, Harvard University

Before the man was deposed, Egyptian President Mohamed Morsi was roundly derided for ramrodding through a new constitution that would have, as his critics charged, made Egypt into an illiberal theocracy. Of special consternation was its second article, which declared that "Islam is the religion of the state and Arabic its official language. Principles of Islamic Sharia are the principal source of legislation." But when Egypt's next constitution, shepherded in by the military and ratified as Morsi stood trial, was found to contain nearly-identical language, the bells of discontent were not rung quite so loud.

Meanwhile, Western nations were recently involved in rewriting the Iraqi and Afghani constitutions, both of which prominently enshrined the position of Islam. Does this analysis affirm the warning that "the elevation of Iranian-style theocrats," as one critical academic put it at the time, would undo the democratic order?

Here, the familiar chiding about correlation and causation need be remembered. Between the high-minded sphere of constitutional design and actual, day-to-day impact on residents lies the apparatus of censors, judges, and policemen who modulate constitutional demands and translate them for the common man. What constitutions prescribe and what bureaucracies end up dealing out can be quite different. Though constitutionally secular, Indonesia has strong anti-blasphemy laws and government-sanctioned persecution against religious minorities.

Academics have also proposed explanations for these Islamic provisions that could complicate matters. So-called "repugnancy clauses," which invalidate laws judged contradictory to Islam and are perhaps the strongest endorsements of religion, are thought to have originated with British rule of India, when the imperial government gave itself the power to overrule legislation "repugnant to the laws of England." And it is often the relatively liberal regimes that introduce Islamist provisions, like Egyptian President Anwar Sadat did in the country's 1971 constitution, probably in an attempt to consolidate power and legitimize themselves before conservatives.

Nonetheless, as the rash of revolution in the Middle East is sure to be followed by a rash of constitution drafting, it's important to know the crowd-pleasers, like acknowledging Islam to be the religion of the state, from the more serious clauses that require all legislation or judicial decisions to have religious approval.

Imagine if Goldilocks were to go constitution-picking. She would settle on something not too theocratic, not too secular. In the Muslim world, that may be just right.

Sample Essay 1 based on Reading / Analysis / Writing Scoring Rubric

INTRODUCTION	
1 Thesis statement (topic sentence)	In response to "Islamic states and democracy", writer Idrees M. Kahloon argues that growing reliance on religion in the Muslim countries is an attempt to preserve and even consolidate power by the rulers of the countries.
	(Title + the author's name + the central argument) ✓Demonstrates thorough comprehension of the source text ✓Shows an understanding of the text's central idea ✓Includes a skillful introduction
2 Supporting detail	His article "Are democracy and constitutional Islam at odds?" is effectively built upon through the contemplation of major modern Islamic countries, compelling published indices, and historical background.
	✓Makes skillful use of textual evidence (quotations, paraphrases or both)
3 Analysis of the thesis & supporting details	Idrees' overall purpose in writing this article appears to be to draw attention towards not impeccable unification of religion and democracy, in which sense his article is persuasive to broad non-Muslim audience.
	✓Offers an insightful analysis of the source text ✓Offers a well-considered evaluation of the author's use of evidence, reasoning, stylistic and persuasive elements.
BODY PARAGRAPH 1	
4 Contrasting point (topic sentence)	In his introduction, Idrees starts with the former convicted Egyptian President Mohamed Morsi, who, according to his critics, made "Egypt into an illiberal theocracy."

5 Analysis of the thesis & supporting details	Idrees utilizes this real-world case to later support his argument by convincingly revealing the fact that Egypt's next constitution was "shepherded" by the military. Such a phrase forces the reader to question that constitutional Islam could be fabricated based on secular-hypocrite motivation opposed to religious doctrine. By delivering this actual incidence, the author leads the reader with more credence to his view.
	✓ Offers an insightful analysis of the source text and demonstrates a sophisticated understanding of the analytical task. ✓ Offers a thorough, well-considered evaluation of the author's use of evidence, reasoning, and/or stylistic and persuasive elements, and/or feature(s) of the student's own choosing.

BODY PARAGRAPH 2

6 Central idea	Followed by his analysis on what motivates rulers in some Muslim countries to adopt religious clauses in constitutions, Idrees further solidifies his argument, bringing academic researches into his analytic argument. He now elaborates the practical effects of constitutional declarations of Islam. As an example, Idrees employs "Islamic Constitutions Index" developed by Dawood I. Ahmed. The index scale shows interactions between religion and democracy among Muslim countries such as public morality, rights, legislation, and the judiciary. By introducing this published academic research, Idrees's analysis gains competent evidence to back up his argument. Using the stratified Muslim states' level of democracy, civil right protections, and how modestly or strongly coerce religious clause into their constitutions ensure the reader to accept the facts that he presents without prejudice. At the end of academic analysis, he concludes that "On average, constitutions with higher measures of Islamic provisions in their constitutions are associated with worse scores in The Economist Intelligence Unit's democracy index, Freedom House's civil liberties ratings, World Economic Forum's gender gap index, and the Pew Research Foundation's index of government restrictions on religion." His reliance on the usage of academic and the officially released indices is insightful in that a subject like religion is very debatable and complicate issue that could easily loose support from either side or fall away from the author's original intentionn.

6 Central idea	✓Shows an understanding of the text's central idea(s) and of most important details and how they interrelate, demonstrating a comprehensive understanding of the text.
BODY PARAGRAPH 3	
7 Central Idea	Finally, Idrees encourages the reader to view this less impressive correlation between religion and democracy in Muslim countries from a broader perspective.
	✓Includes a precise central claim.
8 Supporting detail	He introduces Western nations' involvement in rewriting the Iraqi and Afghani constitutions. He also warns that between what constitutions prescribe and how the constitutional provisions are practiced in actual, day-to-day lives are quite different. He further suggests that we should factor in historical origins such as "repugnancy clauses" arose from the British rule of India.
	✓Makes skillful use of textual evidence (quotations, paraphrases, or both), demonstrating a complete understanding of the source text.
9 Analysis of the thesis & supporting details	His series of elaboration reflects the matter of complexity, limitations of our understanding, and instability of foolproof analysis of this complicate issue. Although his resort to academic indices has its own merit to show credible percentages, figures and data, functional ethos in mainstream, We are unable to quantify Muslim states solely using the data or statistics, says the author. In this regards, his judicious analytic inclusion of historical view and other interpretation requires us to evaluate this article without simple minded reaction.
	✓The response demonstrates a consistent use of precise word choice. The response maintains a formal style and objective tone. ✓Contains relevant, sufficient, and strategically chosen support for claim(s) or point(s) made

Ch. 1 Ch. 2 Ch. 3 Ch. 4 Ch. 5 Ch. 6 Ch. 7 Ch. 8 Ch. 9 Ch. 10

	CONCLUSION
10 Restatement of the central claim	To sum up, idress's analytical skills that encompass academic indices, historical aspects, and reasoning greatly appeal to the reader. He cogently initiated his argument by revealing that the religion in the Muslim countries is being exploited in an attempt to preserve and even consolidate power by the rulers of the countries. He later leads the reader to view the issue with deeper insight. Therefore, it is clear that his argument is exceptionally persuasive in dealing with such a hotly debatable issue.
	✓Includes a skillful introduction and conclusion. ✓The response demonstrates a deliberate and highly effective progression of ideas both within paragraphs and throughout the essay.

Ch. 1

Ch. 2

Ch. 3

Ch. 4

Ch. 5

Ch. 6

Ch. 7

Ch. 8

Ch. 9

Ch. 10

Transitional Phrase Practice

Please read the transitional phrases and the example sentences below.
Using the same phrase, create your own sentence in the practice line.
Each sentence does not have to be related to each other.

Topic: "Not everything that is learned is contained in books." **?**

1	Phrase	A Quick Interjection
	Original Sentence	Before the man was deposed, Egyptian President Mohamed Morsi was roundly derided for ramrodding through a new constitution that would have, as his critics charged, made Egypt into an illiberal theocracy.
	Example	I, with a humongous dream of becoming Luis Armstrong incarnate, got my first job as a sub-music teacher, after moving to Vancouver.
	Practice	
2	Phrase	Inversion
	Original Sentence.	Of special consternation was its second article, which declared that "Islam is the religion of the state and Arabic its official language.
	Example	Of a crucial difference was Luis Armstrong's performance skills, which could blow audiences away.
	Practice	
3	Phrase	~ , both of which…
	Original Sentence.	Meanwhile, Western nations were recently involved in rewriting the Iraqi and Afghani constitutions, both of which prominently enshrined the position of Islam.
	Example	Luis Armstrong studied his predecessors like Duke Ellington and Billy Strayhorn, both of whom prominently enshrined their styles into Jazz.
	Practice	
4	Phrase	So-called "…," which invalidate laws judged contradictory to
	Original Sentence.	So-called "repugnancy clauses," which invalidate laws judged contradictory to Islam and are perhaps the strongest endorsements of religion, are thought to have originated with British rule of India, when the imperial government gave itself the power to overrule legislation "repugnant to the laws of England."

Example		The book so-called "A rise from ashes" invalidates the law of gravity, contradictory to Newton, I, just like the main character in the novel, will rise again.
Practice		

5	Phrase	~ probably in an attempt to consolidate power and legitimize ~.
	Original Sentence	And it is often the relatively liberal regimes that introduce Islamist provisions, like Egyptian President Anwar Sadat did in the country's 1971 constitution, probably in an attempt to consolidate power and legitimize themselves before conservatives.
	Example	In an attempt to consolidate my dream and legitimize myself before my father, I took modern music as my major.
	Practice	
6	Phrase	Nonetheless, ~
	Original Sentence	Nonetheless, as the rash of revolution in the Middle East is sure to be followed by a rash of constitution drafting,
	Example	Nonetheless, my work ethic has never abandoned me, or he it. Success is sure to be followed by struggle to survive.
	Practice	it's important to know the crowd-pleasers,
7	Phrase	It's important to know the crowd-pleasers, ~
	Original Sentence	It's important to know the crowd-pleasers, like acknowledging Islam to be the religion of the state,
	Example	It's important to know the lives of crowd-pleasers, like Justin Bieber, is handsomely manufactured artist, if you could call himself an artist.
	Practice	

8	Phrase	Imagine if Goldilocks …
	Original Sentence	Imagine if Goldilocks were to go constitution-picking.
	Example	Imagine if Goldilocks were on my career. I could truly have found what I would love to do it for free and have become financially and socially acknowledged.
	Practice	

SAMPLE ESSAY 2

Essay Prompt

As you read the passage below, consider how Lily K. Calcagnini uses

♦ evidence, such as facts or examples, to support claims.

♦ reasoning to develop ideas and to connect claims and evidence.

♦ stylistic or persuasive elements, such as word choice or appeals to emotion, to add power to the ideas expressed.

Adopted from Lily K. Calcagnini *"Fashion marketing moves from billboards to museum displays"* © November 20, 2015 The Crimson, Harvard University

Last October, LVMH allocated $143 million to found a private museum of contemporary art for its Louis Vuitton Foundation, and commissioned architect Frank Gehry to design and construct it in Paris's Bois de Boulogne. Even for the multinational conglomerate that runs Louis Vuitton, Moët, Hennessy, and 66 other luxury goods companies—all of which you've definitely heard of—this is a considerable investment worth investigating.

What merits a price tag of $143 million? <u>In part,</u> social capital. When prompted to explain why he wished to open the Louis Vuitton Foundation, Bernard Arnault, the CEO of LVMH,said, "We wanted to present Paris with an extraordinary space for art and culture, and demonstrate daring and emotion by entrusting Frank Gehry with the construction of an iconic building for the 21st century."

Indeed, Arnault was able to successfully build his museum on a plot of land that had previously been denied to several other land developers. While these competitors wished to construct office buildings and business centers, Arnault was granted control of the land because his proposition was deemed to be a noble endeavor to create a public work.
But in a city that already boasts high concentrations of both art and culture, this was an ambitious—maybe even superfluous—undertaking.

It's clear to me that the goal of creating a rich, new ground for cultural discovery was only of secondary importance to Arnault. Though the museum has staged several provoking shows recently, in its opening weeks it showed nothing more than a condensed version of Arnault's private collection.

It is no secret that newer fashion labels have begun to outmode Louis Vuitton, the oldest member of the LVMH conglomerate. In tying the brand's name to a new museum that is sleek, beautiful, and houses millions of dollars worth of art, Arnault intended to reposition and revive the label.

Indeed, the curatorial board explains that their initial goal was not necessarily to draw crowds to the museum's art, but rather to its stunning architecture. That is to say, the artwork created by third parties was at first marketed as less important than the architectural artwork, commissioned by LVMH and bearing the name of one of its child companies.

In so doing, the museum has begun to focus more on mounting provoking art shows, borrowing important works from other famous institutions all over the world. Fashion-Arbiter Arnault has thus established, to some extent, that couture tastemakers are akin to their fine arts counterparts.
In fact, Arnault isn't alone in his ambitiously successful antics. And in the case of Miuccia Prada—the creative director behind the brands Prada and Miu Miu—the endeavor does not stem from a need to reposition her brands at all.

A long-time art collector and enthusiast, Prada's decision to open the Fondazione Prada museum derives simply from a confidence in her own taste in fine art as a designer of fine clothing. In tandem with her husband, Patrizio Bertelli, and architect Rem Koolhaas, she has spent the past seven years designing a campus of ten buildings that boasts over 120,000 square feet of exhibition space; an innovative mixture of dilapidated, ancient aesthetic and modern, minimalist architecture; and amenities like a state-of-the-art movie theater, courtyard, restaurant, and an outdoor pavilion for temporary exhibitions.

It is no surprise that arbiters of haute couture taste successfully intermingle the worlds of high fashion clothing and fine art. At the Metropolitan Museum of Art in New York City, there exists an entire subdivision dedicated to doing just that. The Metropolitan's Costume Institute, in tandem with Anna Wintour, mounts a humongous fashion exhibit each year that blurs the line between fashion and fine art in much the same way. In 2011, the museum launched its exhibit in honor of designer Alexander McQueen, and when the exhibit singlehandedly attracted more foot traffic than any other in the museum's history, it was clear that museumgoers and fashionistas alike had been aching to see the two industries overlap.

Though endeavors like these legitimize fashion <u>as a mode of</u> artistic production, they also render haute couture inaccessible to the masses. Museums showcase things that are untouchable, difficult to parse, and furthermore things that cannot be owned. Though naming a museum of contemporary art after Louis Vuitton ties the brand to culture, the effect is more complex.

Additionally, museums physically separate consumers from clothing. Though I'm already alienated by the four-figured price tag on a Chanel dress, I feel even more unworthy of owning it when that dress must be protected from my touch by glass cases and security ropes.

Though I seriously believe that fashion belongs in museums, it seems that this is not the most effective marketing tactic. <u>However, there does seem to be a way to create museums solely dedicated to clothes that is not alienating, but rather inviting.</u>

Valentino Garavani, owner and designer of the eponymous high-end label, has done so by founding a museum that won't cost him any overhead. In 2011, Garavani and his partner Giancarlo Giammetti launched the Valentino Garavani Virtual Museum, a website and accompanying downloadable applet that provides viewers with unlimited, free access to 50 years of the label's haute couture archives. Featuring cutting-edge, immersive 3-D, the virtual museum allows anyone to interactively explore over 5,000 dresses—their cut, materials, history, and production information.

In comparison to the Louis Vuitton Foundation, Valentino's virtual gallery seems much more honest. LVMH's new museum may indeed be a beautiful gift to the art world and a lovely amenity for Parisians, but as a surreptitious marketing attempt, it is ultimately nothing more than sponsored content.

And while The Fondazione Prada purports only to add to its foundress's empire, I'm interested to see how its opening affects the revenue of the clothing brand that bears her name.

Sample Essay 2 based on Reading / Analysis / Writing Scoring Rubric

INTRODUCTION	
1 Thesis statement (topic sentence)	In the article *"Fashion marketing moves from billboards to museum displays"* Lily K. Calcagnini asserts that although fashion belongs in museums, fashion tycoons such as Bernard Arnault, the CEO of LVMH or Miuccia Prada are mainly motivated by a selfish acts in founding fashion museum that affects the revenue of the clothing brand that bears their name.
	(Title + the author's name + the central argument) ✓Demonstrates thorough comprehension of the source text ✓Shows an understanding of the text's central idea ✓Includes a skillful introduction
2 Analysis of the thesis & supporting details	Lily reasons her analysis by presenting both her experience after visiting the Louis Vuitton museum and the speculation hinged on the Metropolitan's Costume Institute's exhibition. Her final example of the Valentino Garavani Virtual Museum convincingly juxtaposes how fashion industry can be ideally converted into a widely accessible museum instead of means to boost revenue of the fashion brands. Using this analytical technique, Lily persuades her audience and let them evaluate the issue from critics' view.
	✓Offers an insightful analysis of the source text ✓Offers a well-considered evaluation of the author's use of evidence, reasoning, stylistic and persuasive elements.

Ch. 1
Ch. 2
Ch. 3
Ch. 4
Ch. 5
Ch. 6
Ch. 7
Ch. 8
Ch. 9
Ch. 10

BODY PARAGRAPH 1	
3 Central Idea	Lily initiates her analysis by questioning the motivation of LVMH that it found a private museum of contemporary art in Paris.
	✓Includes a precise central claim.
4 Supporting detail	In describing a series of suspicion and discrepancies between what she observed at the museum and the motives of the CEO of LVMH, Bernard Arnault, she debunks the genuine purpose of founding the museum.
	✓Offers a thorough, well-considered evaluation of the author's use of persuasive elements, and/or feature(s) of the student's own choosing.
5 Analysis of the thesis & supporting details	Like Sherlock Holms creates deductive reasoning at a crime scene, Lily invites her audience to unscramble the mystery. In front of Lily, Arnault becomes alleged criminal with a lack of alibi. Using such a tantalizing opening, the author's approach to this sort of investigative Journalism lays out with full of reasoning and projection, personal anecdote, and other similar case studies. Lily's investigation is furthered by her assertion that LVMH is losing its ground as newer fashion labels have begun to outmode its brand like Louis Vuitton in high fashion. Lily claims that "the museum has begun to focus more on mounting provoking art shows, borrowing important works from other famous institutions all over the world." She persuades the reader that this supposedly public museum at the heart of Paris can't be the museum that all people think. She fires up against Arnault that he has no other intention but revive the label of his company by founding a private museum.

6 Analysis of the thesis & supporting details	✓Offers an insightful analysis of the source text and demonstrates a sophisticated understanding of the analytical task. ✓Offers a thorough, well-considered evaluation of the author's use of evidence, reasoning, and/or stylistic and persuasive elements, and/or feature(s) of the student's own choosing. ✓Contains relevant, sufficient, and strategically chosen support for claim(s) or point (s) made. ✓Focuses consistently on those features of the text that are most relevant to addressing the task.
	BODY PARAGRAPH 2
7 Central idea	Lily brings up another example into her investigative analysis: Prada.
8 Supporting detail	She starts with Prada's claim that "she endeavors her ambitions, not stemming from her need to invigorate her brands but from her confidence in her taste in fine art, which drove her to boasts her personal tastes in over 120,000 square feet of exhibition space.
	✓Makes skillful use of textual evidence (quotations, paraphrases, or both), demonstrating a complete understanding of the source text.

9 Analysis of the thesis & supporting details	Throughout the article, Lily unrolls Prada's tainted assertion to open the Fondazione Prada museum. Lily makes an insightful rebuttal at the end of her article "while The Fondazione Prada purports only to add to its foundress's empire, I'm interested to see how its opening affects the revenue of the clothing brand that bears her name." Her word choice clarifies the intention of Prada museum even without letting the reader to weigh credibility.
	✓Offers a thorough, well-considered evaluation of the author's use of evidence, reasoning, and/or stylistic and persuasive elements, and/or feature(s) of the student's own choosing.

<table>
<tr><td colspan="2" align="center">BODY PARAGRAPH 3</td></tr>
</table>

10 Central Idea	Finally, Lily makes efficient use of personal experience she had at the LVMH museum.
11 Supporting detail	To rivet her audience's attention, she exemplifies the collections: "four-figured price tag on a Chanel dress protected by the glass". Her comments on the collections express the symbolism of Amault's resilience to preserve his revenue.
	✓Makes skillful use of textual evidence (quotations, paraphrases, or both), demonstrating a complete understanding of the source text.
12 Analysis of the thesis & supporting details	Her analytical strategy is definitely an appeal to emotion, forcing the audience to directly distinguish Armault and Prada's false claims and the museum's single purpose in reality: a marketing tool. Alternately, Lily proposes the reader to observe Valentino Garavani Virtual Museum in comparison to that of Prada or Amault. She tells the reader Valentino's 3-D Virtual Museum allows anyone can explore over 5,000 dresses and many associate information. This direct comparison by Lily suggests us to weigh why her analysis should be viewed with credence.
	✓The response demonstrates a consistent use of precise word choice. The response maintains a formal style and objective tone. ✓Contains relevant, sufficient, and strategically chosen support for claim(s) or point (s) made.

	CONCLUSION
13 Restatement of the central claim	All in all, her sorts of investigative journal style article fully displays her analytical skills like the way Sherolock Holms does in his detective story, using deductive reasoning, personal experience, or juxtaposition between circumstances and characters. In that sense, her article rivets the audience's heart.
	✓Includes a skillful introduction and conclusion. ✓The response demonstrates a deliberate and highly effective progression of ideas both within paragraphs and throughout the essay.

Transitional Phrase Practice

Please read the transitional phrases and the example sentences below.
Using the same phrase, create your own sentence in the practice line.
Each sentence does not have to be related to each other.

Topic: The widespread use of the internet has given people access to information on a level never experienced before. How does this increase in the availability of information influence life in today's world?

1	Phrase	What merits ~? In part, ~ .
	Original Sentence.	What merits a price tag of $143 million? In part, social capital.
	Example	What merits Internet ? In part, an effective response to growing privacy crisis or cybercrime.
	Practice	
2	Phrase	While ~,
	Original Sentence.	While these competitors wished to construct office buildings and business centers, Arnault was granted control of the land because his proposition was deemed to be a noble endeavor to create a public work.
	Example	While Internet has shaped our world, developing new industries and technologies at an explosive speed, we also aware dangers we face within it.
	Practice	
3	Phrase	It's clear to me that ~
	Original Sentence.	It's clear to me that the goal of creating a rich, new ground for cultural discovery was only of secondary importance to Arnault.
	Example	It is clear to me that because modern security issue is so paramount, characterizing internet as any other great inventions is too dangerous.
	Practice	

4	Phrase	Rather, … by reinvigorating …and thus claiming...
	Original Sentence.	<u>Rather,</u> Bernard Arnault invested almost $1.5 million in his own brand <u>by reinvigorating</u> the name of Louis Vuitton <u>and thus claiming</u> ownership of the art world in the name of high fashion.
	Example	Rather, our shared perspective on cybercrime—especially cyberbully among SNS users—find no effective and direct solutions and causes growing humanitarian concerns, and thus fleeing safe haven to majority SNS users.
	Practice	
5	Phrase	In tying …, Arnault intended to …
	Original Sentence.	In tying the brand's name to a new museum that is sleek, beautiful, and houses millions of dollars worth of art, Arnault intended to reposition and revive the label.
	Example	In tying diversity to collaborative sprit, we can promote inclusion and add value to cyber world, treating it as a valuable single global community.
	Practice	
6	Phrase	<u>In so doing,</u> …
	Original Sentence.	<u>In so doing,</u> the museum has begun to focus more on mounting provoking art shows, borrowing important works from other famous institutions all over the world.
	Example	In so doing, Facebook can provide support to cyber-attack victims, funding to those especially parents-unaccompanied children.
	Practice	
7	Phrase	… derives simply from …
	Original Sentence.	A long-time art collector and enthusiast, Prada's decision to open the Fondazione Prada museum <u>derives simply from</u> a confidence in her own taste in fine art as a designer of fine clothing.
	Example	Facebook's recent decision to fund the middle eastern refuge children drives simply from a confidence in its brand name solidification.
	Practice	

8	Phrase	… blurs the line between …
	Original Sentence	The Metropolitan's Costume Institute, in tandem with Anna Wintour, mounts a humongous fashion exhibit each year that blurs the line between fashion and fine art in much the same way.
	Example	We are heading into the world that blurs the line between reality and virtual reality.
	Practice	
9	Phrase	… as a mode of …
	Original Sentence	Though endeavors like these legitimize fashion as a mode of artistic production, they also render haute couture inaccessible to the masses.
	Example	SNS as a mode of main communication has transferred the world using landline telephone at its lowest level.
	Practice	
10	Phrase	However, there does seem to be a way to … that is not …, but rather …
	Original Sentence	However, there does seem to be a way to create museums solely dedicated to clothes that is not alienating, but rather inviting.
	Example	However, there does seem to be a way to create human connection that does not require to rub your mouse vigorously, but rather physically contacting other human being.
	Practice	

SAMPLE ESSAY 3

Essay Prompt

As you read the passage below, consider how **Shubhankar Chhokra** uses

♦ evidence, such as facts or examples, to support claims.

♦ reasoning to develop ideas and to connect claims and evidence.

♦ stylistic or persuasive elements, such as word choice or appeals to emotion, to add power to the ideas expressed.

Adopted from Shubhankar Chhokra "Obama's Disillusioned Doctrine" © March 25, 2016
The Crimson, Harvard University

Next month's cover story for The Atlantic is the final installment of Jeffrey Goldberg's series of foreign policy interviews with President Obama, a conversation that has spanned all eight years of his presidency. If each interview has served us a taste of what the most powerful man on earth was thinking at the time, then this final piece—an essay, not a transcript like the others—was the whole meal start to finish.

As the name of the essay suggests, Goldberg's piece lays out The Obama Doctrine, the organizing principle behind the momentous foreign policy of a man whose unlikely rise to the American presidency often overshadows his far more unlikely rise to the seat of Commander in Chief. Here's a man who went from being the Illinois State Senator to the commander of our armed forces in a mere four years—quite a remarkable feat.

No less remarkable a feat than Goldberg's essay itself, "The Obama Doctrine" isn't conjecture from historians poring through State of the Union transcripts decades later, but rather the words of a sitting president. The gravity of this essay cannot be overstated. In it, we see Obama reflect on specific decisions—not striking Assad, pivoting to Asia, intervening in Libya—only in order to make broader claims about his presidency, to situate himself historically among the liberal interventionists, the internationalists, the isolationists, and the realists.

Out of these schools, Obama says he is closest to the realists, believing that "we can't, at any given moment, relieve all the world's misery." He says, "We have to choose where we can make a real impact." That is why, he says, he stood quietly as Putin invaded Crimea in 2014, a core interest for Russia but hardly one for the United States. That is why he reneged on his 2012 promise to intervene in Syria after Assad deployed chemical weapons on his own people.

But not even the most sympathetic Obama supporter could go through Goldberg's piece and chalk his decisions these past eight years up to realism. Throughout the interview, one observes an insuperable level of disillusionment in our president. He laments the diplomatic ties and obligations he has to tolerate because of mere tradition—the misogynistic Saudis, the autocratic Turks, Bibi Netanyahu's exhausting condescension.

Obama also deplores the Western allies who ride on American coat tails, a claim that would be understandable if he at least took part of the blame for his missteps. In perhaps the most irritating line of the entire interview, Obama comments on the failure to stabilize Libya: "When I go back and I ask myself what went wrong, there's room for criticism, because I had more faith in the Europeans, given Libya's proximity, being invested in the follow-up."

"There's room for criticism because I had more faith in the Europeans"—no line better betrays this administration's gross misunderstanding of global power dynamics. A true realist—if we are to take Obama's self-identification seriously—understands that free-riding is a negligible price to pay for stability and is moreover an inevitable outcome of coalition diplomacy. If our president's sensibilities on fairness are enough cause to retreat, Russia and Iran are eager to eat the costs of free-riding if it means they could fill the lucrative power vacuum we would leave behind.

The most compelling case for the Obama Doctrine—which if not an offshoot of realism, is something more akin to "isolationism with drones and special-ops forces" as one critic calls it—was blown up this week in Brussels along with 34 civilians, in the deadliest act of terrorism in Belgian history. Obama claims that "ISIS is not an existential threat to the United States," rather "climate change is a potential existential threat to the entire world if we don't do something about it." This is jaded Obama at work—recklessly allowing his Weltschmerz to cloud his judgment, choosing more romantic, less controversial battles like climate change and the favorite cause of his first term, the "pivot to Asia."

This is not to discount Obama's likely genuine belief that climate change demands our attention more than terrorism. But **at the root of this claim is not logic,** but a fatigue of the Middle East and a yearning for something new. Obama explains to Goldberg about why he prefers to talk about Asia more than ISIS, "They are not thinking about how to kill Americans," he says. "What they're thinking about is 'How do I get a better education? How do I create something of value?'" This sounds like a man so lustful for hope that he's willing to radically skew his priorities.

Ch. 1
Ch. 2
Ch. 3
Ch. 4
Ch. 5
Ch. 6
Ch. 7
Ch. 8
Ch. 9
Ch. 10

<u>Hope is the Obama doctrine's Achilles' heel.</u> Where Obama does not find hope, he shies away. Where a good leader does not find hope, he is duty-bound to keep looking.

David Frum's takeaway from Goldberg's final essay is that all of us have disappointed Barack Obama—that our Western allies are guilty of free-loading, <u>that Americans are guilty of overestimating the threat of ISIS to the point that out fear devolves into bigotry,</u> and that the entire world just needs to be more realistic. President Obama is probably not wrong about any of this, but he is certainly wrong in expecting others to sympathize with his disappointment.

In what will probably be the most cited line of Goldberg's piece, he quotes the King of Jordan as saying, "I think I believe in American power more than Obama does." Indeed, by the end of this essay, Obama does not seem like a realist, but a man too world-weary to lead, too keen on finding hope to take hopeless situations seriously.

Sample Essay 3 based on Reading / Analysis / Writing Scoring Rubric

	INTRODUCTION
1 Thesis statement (topic-sentence)	Shubhankar Chhokra examines Obama's foreign policy in his article "Obama's Disillusioned Doctrine. Here, Shubhankar addresses concerns of Obama's remarkably unremarkable inactions during his presidency.
	(Title + the author's name + the central argument) ✓Demonstrates thorough comprehension of the source text ✓Shows an understanding of the text's central idea ✓Includes a skillful introduction
2 Analysis of the thesis & supporting details	By examining Obama's overall performance in foreign policy, Shubhankar gives much of the criticism crafted with a persuasive argument, and stylistic elements--solidifying his analysis using the references from critics.
	✓Offers an insightful analysis of the source text ✓Offers a well-considered evaluation of the author's use of evidence, reasoning, stylistic and persuasive elements.
	BODY PARAGRAPH 1
4 Central Idea	To start with, Shubhankar defames "Obama's rise to the seat of Commander in Chief is far more unlikely than the unlikelihood of his rise to the American presidency".
	✓Includes a precise central claim. ✓Makes skillful use of textual evidence (quotations, paraphrases or both)

6 Analysis of the thesis & supporting details	At this point, the audience—especially those who support Obama or Obama Doctrine at least--might ask whether Shubhankar's analysis reflects the truth based upon evidential proof. To substantiate his article, Shubhankar chastises Obama's naïve attachment to a word "hope" and less controversial issues like climate control. By utilizing full of ironic quotes from Obama's speech such as, "That is why he stood quietly as Putin invaded Crimea in 2014". Shubhankar reveals the comprehensive failure of Obama administration's foreign policy patched with mockery and accusation. "We have to choose where we can make a real impact.", after reneging to intervening Syria; "There's room for criticism because I had more faith in the Europeans", after failing to stabilizing Libya; and finally, "ISIS is not an existential threat to the United States," rather "climate change is". These quotes from president Obama persuade the reader to think that outcomes could have been better, than what he did. To garner the audience attention from somewhat a heavy issue like Obama's foreign policy failure, Shubhankar employs various stylistic devise such as juxtaposition, irony, quotation. As an example, he categorizes a potential existential threat to the world and more romantic, less controversial battles like climate change or "pivot to Asia". Within this broad division he persuades the reader how illogical his doctrine has been, how irrational Obama has been in preceding and romanticizing grave world issues.
	✓Offers an insightful analysis of the source text and demonstrates a sophisticated understanding of the analytical task. ✓Offers a thorough, well-considered evaluation of the author's use of evidence, reasoning, and/or stylistic and persuasive elements, and/or feature(s) of the student's own choosing. ✓Contains relevant, sufficient, and strategically chosen support for claim(s) or point(s) made. ✓Focuses consistently on those features of the text that are most relevant to addressing the task.

HARVARD STUDENT ESSAY ANALAYS

Ch. 1

Ch. 2

Ch. 3

Ch. 4

Ch. 5

Ch. 6

Ch. 7

Ch. 8

Ch. 9

Ch. 10

BODY PARAGRAPH 2	
7 Central idea	He then tries to back up his argument by presenting a quote from David Frum."that all of us have disappointed Barack Obama".
	✓ Shows an understanding of the text's central idea(s) and of most important details and how they interrelate, demonstrating a comprehensive understanding of the text.
8 Analysis of the thesis & supporting details	Shubhankar finds president Obama's illogical approach to foreign policy from his fatigue and lighthearted naivety. He, using several quotations from David Frum, reveals what Obama focused on his doctrine. Avoiding issues like "how to kill Americans" and adhering issues like "Asian education" leads the audience to take his side. From Shubhankar's eyes, Obama's denial of ISIS threat by underestimating terrorism, and exaggeration of climate change—which doesn't give us the same level of immediate threat as grave as the one we get from 9/11 or ISIS terrorism—establishes genuine doubt about Obama doctrine, if not a doubt about the president Obama.
	Shubhankar's view on Obama doctrine, although debatable, at least warns the reader who tends to proactively trust Obama. The audience, after reading his article, will definitely open up the eyes to see Obama from a different angel.
	✓ Offers a thorough, well-considered evaluation of the author's use of evidence, reasoning, and/or stylistic and persuasive elements, and/or feature(s) of the student's own choosing. ✓ Contains relevant, sufficient, and strategically chosen support for claim(s) or point(s) made. (Include - statistics- data- official names)

CONCLUSION	
13 Restatement of the central claim	In conclusion, starting from Goldberg's interview and finalizing his argument with a quote from David Frum, Shubahankar renders the audience to observe the genuine failure of Obama doctrine. In an effort to persuade his audience, Shubahnakar didn't seem to be afraid of the supporters of the incumbent president Obama. Rather, he sends a unqualified remarks with full of irony and sarcasm to bolster his analysis. His approach is quintessential because it insightfully protects his argument mainly by articulating how critics believe about the issue. When the issue is on-going, and therefore not enough evidential proof or data is available, probably an ultimate choice to get the reader's attention might be utilizing or touching the emotion with strong voice and word choice.
	✓Includes a skillful introduction and conclusion. ✓The response demonstrates a deliberate and highly effective progression of ideas

Transitional Phrase Practice

Direction
Please read the transitional phrases and the example sentences below.
Using the same phrase, create your own sentence in the practice line.
Each sentence does not have to be related to each other.

Topic:
A company is going to give some money either to support the arts or to protect the environment. Which do you think the company should choose? Use specific reasons and examples to support your answer.

1	Phrase	As the name of the essay suggests, …
	Original Sentence.	As the name of the essay suggests, Goldberg's piece lays out The Obama Doctrine, the organizing principle behind the momentous foreign policy of a man whose unlikely rise to the American presidency often overshadows his far more unlikely rise to the seat of Commander in Chief.
	Example	As the name of the essay suggests, our argument for why a company should invest in the environment over the arts falls into a simple answer: to boost the economy.
	Practice	
2	Phrase	… isn't conjecture from …but rather …
	Original Sentence.	The Obama Doctrine" isn't conjecture from historians poring through State of the Union transcripts decades later, but rather the words of a sitting president.
	Example	A company's fund to the environment, however, shouldn't be based on conjecture, but rather on planning how it will get the money, how much it will actually invest, and to what it will use the fund.
	Practice	
3	Phrase	The gravity of … cannot be overstated. In it, we see … reflect on specific decisions—
	Original Sentence.	The gravity of this essay cannot be overstated. In it, we see Obama reflect on specific decisions—
	Example	The gravity of the investment decision to the environment from private sectors cannot be overstated. In it, we see a proof of contribution, reflect on the public's voice.
	Practice	

4	Phrase	But not even the most sympathetic supporter could go through …
	Original Sentence.	But not even the most sympathetic Obama supporter could go through Goldberg's piece and chalk his decisions these past eight years up to realism.
	Example	But not even the most sympathetic economic supporters could go through the challenges of global warming.
	Practice	
5	Phrase	"There's room for criticism ..
	Original Sentence.	"There's room for criticism because I had more faith in the Europeans"
	Example	There's room for criticism in current environment protection laws. Some claim the rules for environment protection are so long and complex that companies would not understand.
	Practice	
6	Phrase	…if we are to take … seriously--understand that …
	Original Sentence.	A true realist—if we are to take Obama's self-identification seriously—understands that free-riding is a negligible price to pay for stability and is moreover an inevitable outcome of coalition diplomacy.
	Example	If we are to take the global warming issue seriously—understand that current debates have offered nothing but conflicts of interest, private companies will find it very difficult to resist changes.
	Practice	
7	Phrase	The most compelling case for …
	Original Sentence.	The most compelling case for the Obama Doctrine—which if not an offshoot of realism, is something more akin to "isolationism with drones and special-ops forces" as one critic calls it—was blown up this week in Brussels along with 34 civilians, in the deadliest act of terrorism in Belgian history.
	Example	The most compelling case for this argument for why private donors should focus more on the climate change issue is that the government now favors tax breaks for those people.
	Practice	

8	Phrase	… to cloud his judgment, choosing more romantic, less controversial battles like …
	Original Sentence.	This is jaded Obama at work—recklessly allowing his Weltschmerz to cloud his judgment, choosing more romantic, less controversial battles like climate change and the favorite cause of his first term, the "pivot to Asia."
	Example	Some people still believe climate change is more romantic, less controversial issue by clouding their judgment to more instigating issue like ISIS.
	Practice	
9	Phrase	This is not to discount …
	Original Sentence.	This is not to discount Obama's likely genuine belief that climate change demands our attention more than terrorism.
	Example	This is not to discount the gravity of terrorism issues. With all due respect, environment protection also demands our attention.
	Practice	
10	Phrase	But at the root of this claim is not logic,
	Original Sentence.	But at the root of this claim is not logic, but a fatigue of the Middle East and a yearning for something new.
	Example	At the root of this claim is not logic but may find a naïve and fertile ground to disseminate false-claim.
	Practice	
11	Phrase	…is the Achilles' heel.
	Original Sentence.	Hope is the Obama doctrine's Achilles' heel.
	Example	Persuading private companies to sacrifice their profits by entering climate control protocol has been Achilles' heel.
	Practice	

12	Phrase	… to the point that ~
	Original Sentence.	that Americans are guilty of overestimating the threat of ISIS to the point that out fear devolves into bigotry,
	Example	Some third-world-countries' failing to respond to the global climate change protocol is expediting the warming process to the point that we experience flooding in some desert Africa.
	Practice	

SAMPLE ESSAY 4

Essay Prompt

As you read the passage below, consider how Shubhankar Chhokra uses

♦evidence, such as facts or examples, to support claims.

♦reasoning to develop ideas and to connect claims and evidence.
♦stylistic or persuasive elements, such as word choice or appeals to emotion, to add power to the ideas expressed.

Adopted from Shubhankar Chhokra "Recent fruit deregulation bears little fruit" © May 8, 2015
The Crimson, Harvard University

Apples are important. They are lodged in our throats and imprinted on our cell phones. They proxy in for the unspecified fruit Eve gave Adam, and pies made out of them are quintessentially American. My graduating class planted 14 trees of them at our high school, and 30 years from now, we hope to return with spouses and children, hungry for the fruits of our labor. And as I eat this apple, alternating bites with lines of prose, I savor all this historical, cultural, and personal significance even more than its sweet flavor.

Nothing would please me more than writing an article chronicling mankind's fixation with the apple. That says a lot about me. Fortunately for you though, the apple is even more important as a commodity than an artifact, so this is the story of how one fruit might just determine the future of American agriculture.

Earlier this week, the United States Department of Agriculture announced that it's lifting its import restrictions on fresh apples from China. That means starting this month, China—the world's largest producer of apples—can freely enter American markets, selling cheap and low-quality fruit in direct competition with our nation's harvest. American officials are hoping this decision would persuade the Chinese—who only currently import red and golden delicious apples from a handful of states—to loosen their own trade restrictions in good faith.

As China's consumption of American apples is definitely nontrivial, this expectation of requital makes sense. Interestingly, according to President of the Washington Apple Commission Todd Fryhover, Chinese consumers are especially hungry for more Red Delicious apples because their rich, crimson hue represents good fortune in their culture. But flooding American markets with Chinese apples in hope of the reverse is ultimately unfruitful triage for the more pressing problem, one that is closer to home: we just had the largest apple crop in American history and need foreign buyers to compensate for lackluster domestic demand.

<u>Wagering the already problematic American apple industry on faith that China will reciprocate is incredibly short-sighted,</u> especially because we've been unsuccessfully trying to get the nation to relent on its import restrictions for a couple years now. Even if they do, it won't amount to much.
If you've been following the Chinese's apple purchasing closely for the past couple years (like, who hasn't?), you would notice that China doesn't really need American apples.

China purchased its largest shipment of Australian apples just this week, and will start importing from South Africa, where farm labor and manufacturing is much cheaper that in the states, in May. Domestically, China produces nine times as many apples as the US does with lower costs of production, and accordingly exports more apples than it imports by a margin larger than America's entire apple supply. This is all to say the USDA is either lying or kidding itself when it says that it expects China to contribute no more than 0.4% of apples consumed in America.

<u>There are reasons why we haven't welcomed Chinese apples in the past.</u> China's atrocious food safety <u>regulations and pollution problems pose a serious threat to American consumers.</u> **And the USDA initially** barred Chinese apples because they carry invasive pests like the Oriental fruit fly that could destroy entire crops of American apples. These dangers, unlike the government's attitude towards them, haven't changed.

<u>We're on the verge of an apple crisis with some pretty precarious implications on the health of American consumers and livelihoods of American farmers.</u> And as President Obama attempts to fast track the Trans-Pacific Partnership on the coattails of the purportedly infallible "free" trade model, these same issues with the trade balance and safety will emerge in other sectors of the agriculture economy as well. Under the North American Free Trade Agreement just a couple decades ago, the abrupt influx of cheap foreign foodreversed our once impressive agriculture trade surplus and brought hundreds of thousands of farmers to bankruptcy. It looks like we haven't learned from our mistake.

Sample Essay 4 based on Reading / Analysis / Writing Scoring Rubric

	INTRODUCTION	
1 Thesis statement (topic sentence)	Shubhankar Chhokra's article "Recent fruit deregulation bears little fruit" raises concerns about the U.S. government's latest decision to lift the apple import from China.	
	(Title + the author's name + the central argument) ✓ Demonstrates thorough comprehension of the source text ✓ Shows an understanding of the text's central idea ✓ Includes a skillful introduction	
2 Analysis of the thesis & supporting details	The author warns that sticking to the policy will increase the burden to American farmers, while rewarding only China. His article is well organized in his use of the report from USDA, his personal anecdote, appeal to the reader's emotion, and stylistic word choices such as humorous allusions about apple. Shubhankar's reasons through solid, real-world examples also convincingly reveals his purpose of writing.	
	✓ Offers an insightful analysis of the source text ✓ Offers a well-considered evaluation of the author's use of evidence, reasoning, stylistic and persuasive elements.	

BODY PARAGRAPH 1

	BODY PARAGRAPH 1	
3 Central Idea	Shubhankar paints his introduction paragraph with colorful--tinged with humor—veneration to apple. By utilizing a stylish lighthearted pros to his article, he generates great curiosity from the reader about the issue that otherwise could have been a grave and boring trade deficit report.	
	✓ Includes a precise central claim. ✓ Makes skillful use of textual evidence (quotations, paraphrases or both)	

4 Analysis of the thesis & supporting details	Shubhankar elaborates his analysis by elucidating why the recent announcement from the United States Department of Agriculture that it is lifting its import restrictions on fresh apples from china is an irreversible mistake. He argues that, by inferring the quote from President of the Washington Apple Commission Todd Fryhover, the decision will create even greater challenges to American farmers amid "the largest apple crop in American history and need foreign buyers to compensate for lackluster domestic demand." His quote borrowed from Todd Fryhover is very persuasive because a person like him working at the very front line of apple consumption in U.S. can reveal the reality and reflect the author's opinion in his favor. To confront the bureaucracy and raise a sensible objection against its decision requires a simple rule: the utilization and optimization of the public voice. In that sense, Shubahankar empowers his voice by strategically approaching to not only apple's core but also to the issue.
	✓Offers an insightful analysis of the source text and demonstrates a sophisticated un-derstanding of the analytical task. ✓Offers a thorough, well-considered evaluation of the author's use of evidence, rea-soning, and/or stylistic and persuasive elements, and/or feature(s) of the student's own choosing. ✓Contains relevant, sufficient, and strategically chosen support for claim(s) or point (s) made. ✓Focuses consistently on those features of the text that are most relevant to address-ing the task.
BODY PARAGRAPH 2	
5 Central idea	Shubahankar further admonishes the government's decision made on faith that "China will reciprocate" as a myopic and naïve judgment.
	✓Shows an understanding of the text's central idea(s) and of most important details and how they interrelate, demonstrating a comprehensive understanding of the text.

6 Analysis of the thesis & supporting details	Instead of citing the numbers and statistics directly, the author skillfully invites his audience by humorously asking rhetoric question. "if you've been following the Chinese's apple purchasing closely…(like, who hasn't?).". His stylistic approach gives a significant counterweight in presenting his argument. By doing so, his argument adds on weight to the following index, backed by data and logical comparison.
	✓Offers a thorough, well-considered evaluation of the author's use of evidence, reasoning, and/or stylistic and persuasive elements, and/or feature(s) of the student's own choosing. ✓Contains relevant, sufficient, and strategically chosen support for claim(s) or point(s) made. (Include - statistics- data- official names)

BODY PARAGRAPH 3

7 Central idea	Following the through numeric data that explicitly warns the imminent outcome of the decision by USDA, Shubahankar appeals to the reader's emotion.
	✓Shows an understanding of the text's central idea(s) and of most important details and how they interrelate, demonstrating a comprehensive understanding of the text.
8 Analysis of the thesis & supporting details	He articulates the reasons USDA did not approve Chinese fresh apple importation in the past. His word selections such as "atrocious food safety", "pollution problem", or "invasive pests" add extra weight on his argument because the dangers he presents here touches the reader's nerve that can't be simply calculated. The psychological impact the reader received from his argument might disarm any possible debates from the opponents. He says "an apple crisis" or "pretty precarious implication on the health of American". The author's deployment of this psychological implications on the later part of his article juxtaposes with his humorous opening paragraph. His effective analytic strategy that stratifies the issue from humour, data, and psychological revelation provides accurate depiction of the true problems caused by the recent USDA's decision. With all due respect, the core of his analytical skill is saved at the concluding paragraph. He employs several allusions--historical, scientific, and literal—which remind the reader about the importance of apple. In his comical ending, Shubahankar enters the reader's mind without objection.

8 Analysis of the thesis & supporting details	✓Offers a thorough, well-considered evaluation of the author's use of evidence, reasoning, and/or stylistic and persuasive elements, and/or feature(s) of the student's own choosing. ✓Contains relevant, sufficient, and strategically chosen support for claim(s) or point(s) made. (Include - statistics- data- official names)
CONCLUSION	
13 Restatement of the central claim	Overall, Shubahankar's article is well prepared in every angle: from personal anecdote, numeric data from the government, utilization of powerful voice that represents American apple farmers, and stylistic devices such as humorous rhetorical question, allusions he employed throughout the article effectively persuades the reader.
	✓Includes a skillful introduction and conclusion. ✓The response demonstrates a deliberate and highly effective progression of ideas both within paragraphs and throughout the essay.

Transitional Phrase Practice

Direction
Please read the transitional phrases and the example sentences below.
Using the same phrase, create your own sentence in the practice line.
Each sentence does not have to be related to each other.

Topic: In general, people are living longer now. Discuss the causes of this phenomenon

1	Phrase	… is incredibly short-sighted
	Original Sentence	Wagering the already problematic American apple industry on faith that China will reciprocate is incredibly short-sighted
	Example	Describing that human longevity is romance is incredibly short-sighted.
	Practice	
2	Phrase	This is all to say …
	Original Sentence	This is all to say the USDA is either lying or kidding itself when it says that it expects China to contribute no more than 0.4% of apples consumed in America.
	Example	This is all to say that saving millions of lives every year with advanced medical practice means we need to create the same number of extra jobs every year.
	Practice	
3	Phrase	There are reasons why …
	Original Sentence	There are reasons why we haven't welcomed Chinese apples in the past.
	Example	There are reasons why human longevity reduces social and economical development.
	Practice	

4	Phrase	… pose a serious threat
	Original Sentence.	China's atrocious food safety regulations and pollution problems pose a serious threat to American consumers.
	Example	Old people without financial security pose a serious threat to the entire economy.
	Practice	
5	Phrase	We're on the verge of …
	Original Sentence.	We're on the verge of an apple crisis with some pretty precarious implications on the health of American consumers and livelihoods of American farmers.
	Example	We are on the verge of 100-year-old as a median life expectancy.
	Practice	
6	Phrase	The integrity of … does not boil down to …
	Original Sentence.	The integrity of the American economy does not boil down to apple trade.
	Example	Although the integrity of overall economy does not boil down to a job security of a single aged group, they may make social cost far more burdensome.
	Practice	

SAMPLE ESSAY 5

Essay Prompt

As you read the passage below, consider how Sam Danello uses

♦evidence, such as facts or examples, to support claims.

♦reasoning to develop ideas and to connect claims and evidence.
♦stylistic or persuasive elements, such as word choice or appeals to emotion, to add power to the ideas expressed.

Adopted from Sam Danello *"How social media portrays mortality*
" © May 4, 2015 The Crimson, Harvard University

Two Saturdays ago, a 7.8 magnitude earthquake ripped through Nepal, resulting in widespread damage to infrastructure, irreparable harm to historical sites, and, most tragically, the deaths of thousands and thousands of human beings. Such an event should inspire mourning and contemplation—sorrow for the people who lost their lives and gratitude for the lives that we still have. Instead, in the aftermath of the tremors, a different sort of behavior rose up from the rubble. News outlets ran reports of individuals—some tourists and some Nepalese citizens—stopping in front of destroyed buildings for quick selfies. Here was one sort of earthquake response: Survey the tragic scene, take a smiling photo, and then skip off in the opposite direction. If social media glorifies life—capturing our most intimate moments and recording our funniest jokes—then it does the opposite for death. In Nepal, the pressure of social media gave users an incentive to turn a deep and wide human tragedy into a shallow snapshot.

To a certain degree, you can blame the photographers. A tactful person should have enough respect to avoid behavior that reduces a death into a tagged detail.
Yet a larger, and more disconcerting, criticism of the selfie-behavior that emerged out of the Nepal earthquake has to do with the nature of social media itself.
By displaying nothing more than instances of frivolity, by encouraging users to disguise themselves inside a sunny-beach persona, social media prevents the acknowledgement of deeper emotions, such as grief.

Against a background of party photos and emojis, mortality loses all of its defining gravitas. The deceased become abject and even absurd—they simply can't coexist with this sepia-tinted world in which every comment is an inside joke.

Put it this way: There is nothing more unsettling than the Facebook profile of a dead teenager.
I think the uneasy feeling derives from the lightheartedness of the content that dominates any social media platform. There are airy "lol" comments; there are witty photo captions.
There is rarely, if ever, a reminder that this person—this very same smiling person—is fragile enough to die.

How can you reconcile social media's giddy artificiality with death's stone-cold reality? How can you connect a corpse to a profile picture?

I'd like to provide an answer, but I sense these questions are rhetorical—Facebook simply lacks the tools to chronicle death

That's why it feels slightly invasive to log onto the profile of a dead person; that's why you wince when you read trivial comments on the same profile, knowing all the time that the commenter is no longer around to make such banal remarks.

Over the past several months, I have often described social media as a sort of illusion. There is the illusion of popularity, the illusion of philanthropy, and the illusion ofsubstance.
In some ways, however, I think that the mortality-defying effects of social media are the most illusory and therefore the most dangerous. The more time you spend on Facebook, engaging with the social detritus of your friends, former friends, and hope-to-be friends, the more you sidestep the most central truth of your own existence.

Everyone dies one day, but on Facebook, all you can see is eternal bacchanalia and laughter.

The easiest recommendation is to unplug your life and spend more time appreciating the fragile beauty of real things. The fact that something—a season, a flower, or a person—is temporary, essentially makes that something more valuable.

But realizing that everyone, myself included, needs social media for practical life purposes, a more realistic suggestion revolves around mindfulness.

"Mindfulness"—this may sound like an empty word, but I believe that it encapsulates the overarching message that I've tried to drive home throughout a semester of column writing.

Ch. 1

Ch. 2

Ch. 3

Ch. 4

Ch. 5

Ch. 6

Ch. 7

Ch. 8

Ch. 9

Ch. 10

The Internet is powerful, practical, and practically powerful. You need to use it for these reasons.

However, you need to use the Internet well, which requires significant reflection. Think hard before you click to open a new tab; philosophize as you sign into Facebook.

Everything about the Internet conspires to sweep you away into an arcade world of images and sounds, but you must resist in order to maintain your identity and willpower.

After all, your humanity is based in this resistance—and in the wonderful freedom that follows.

Sample Essay 5 based on Reading / Analysis / Writing Scoring Rubric

	INTRODUCTION
1 Thesis statement (topic sentence)	In his article *"How social media portrays mortality"* writer Sam Danello argues that humanity should be preserved and not be compromised in Facebook.
	(Title + the author's name + the central argument) ✓Demonstrates thorough comprehension of the source text ✓Shows an understanding of the text's central idea ✓Includes a skillful introduction
2 Supporting detail	He insightfully elaborates his argument by reflecting the recent earthquake devastated Nepal.
	✓Makes skillful use of textual evidence (quotations, paraphrases or both)
3 Analysis of the thesis & supporting details	Without having a measured statistics or data to support his argument, his introspection touches up a quintessential question resides in Facebook.
	✓Offers an insightful analysis of the source text ✓Offers a well-considered evaluation of the author's use of evidence, reasoning, stylistic and persuasive elements.
	BODY PARAGRAPH 1
4 Contrasting point (topic sentence)	Using the recent tragic earthquake in Nepal, Sam discredits Social network Facebook by pointing out its nature : "if social media glorifies life…then it does the opposite for death."
	✓Includes a precise central claim. ✓Makes skillful use of textual evidence (quotations, paraphrases or both)

5 Analysis of the thesis & supporting details	He blames how Facebook turns a deep human tragedy into a shallow snapshot. Sam admonishes the reader it is not to blame the photographers who "reduce a death into a tagged detail, next to emojji". He finds that Facebook, cheerleading sunny-beach persona, party photos and witty jokes, simply does not allow coexistence with deeper emotions, such as grief, mortality. Rather, the deceased become absurd in Facebook. Sam coerces the reader to question whether we are not haunted by social media's illusion: "the illusion of popularity, the illusion of philanthropy, and the illusion of substance" He did not use statistics or analytical skills because even by the modest standards of human intellect, everybody knows that we should never tolerate treating mortality with frivolous sticky note with happy smile. His persuasion to his reader on the central argument is so powerful and insightful because it is not to ask what is wrong or what is right, but it ultimately asks who we are, painting Facebook only to be acknowledged. Sam's article impresses the reader because his view on the issue is the one that can't be compromised or debated.
	✓Offers an insightful analysis of the source text and demonstrates a sophisticated understanding of the analytical task. ✓Offers a thorough, well-considered evaluation of the author's use of evidence, reasoning, and/or stylistic and persuasive elements, and/or feature(s) of the student's own choosing. ✓Contains relevant, sufficient, and strategically chosen support for claim(s) or point(s) made. ✓Focuses consistently on those features of the text that are most relevant to addressing the task.

BODY PARAGRAPH 2

6 Central idea	Sam asks his reader to unplug Facebook for a while and "spend more time appreciating the fragile beauty of real things."
	✓Shows an understanding of the text's central idea(s) and of most important details and how they interrelate, demonstrating a comprehensive understanding of the text.

7 Analysis of the thesis & supporting details	He reasons that something more valuable are "a flower, a person or a season" He admits he also uses Facebook for a practical reason and that we cannot avoid ourselves from being inherently self-serving. But Sam suggests us to be judicious before click on a mouse, before we post something on Facebook because whatever we wrote mindlessly can turns into a significant harms to others.
	✓ Offers a thorough, well-considered evaluation of the author's use of evidence, reasoning, and/or stylistic and persuasive elements, and/or feature(s) of the student's own choosing. ✓ Contains relevant, sufficient, and strategically chosen support for claim(s) or point(s) made. (Include - statistics- data- official names)

BODY PARAGRAPH 3

8 Central Idea	In his article, Sam uses strikingly impressive words "Put it this way: There is nothing more unsettling than the Facebook profile of a dead teenager.".
	✓ Includes a precise central claim.
9 Analysis of the thesis & supporting details	Sam wants to find out why social media content has to be that way, and how we are mindlessly following or even wish to be acknowledged in the exactly same way as Facebook drives us to be. Sam's appeal to emotion mirrors the general human being's innate human nature. That is why he could easily penetrate the reader's mind—even to some who are not disillusioned to Facebook, who believe what it is shown on Facebook is the ultimate existence.
	✓ The response demonstrates a consistent use of precise word choice. The response maintains a formal style and objective tone. ✓ Contains relevant, sufficient, and strategically chosen support for claim(s) or point(s) made.

CONCLUSION	
10 Restatement of the central claim	His strong word choices, "Everyone dies one day, but on Facebook, all you can see is eternal bacchanalia and laughter.". are very heartfelt, very human touch to the issue encompassing all his arguments, his view, urges. His appeal to the reader's emotion relevantly and cogently betrays the reality of Social media and how we become get used to it.
	✓ Includes a skillful introduction and conclusion. ✓ The response demonstrates a deliberate and highly effective progression of ideas both within paragraphs and throughout the essay.

Transitional Phrase Practice

Direction

Please read the transitional phrases and the example sentences below.
Using the same phrase, create your own sentence in the practice line.
Each sentence does not have to be related to each other.

Topic: Is it better to enjoy your money when you earn it or is it better to save your money for some time in the future?

1	Phrase	If …then it does the opposite …
	Original Sentence.	If social media glorifies life—capturing our most intimate moments and recording our funniest jokes—then it does the opposite for death.
	Example	If reckless spending gives us enjoyment at present, it gives us the opposite in the future.
	Practice	
2	Phrase	To a certain degree, …
	Original Sentence.	To a certain degree, you can blame the photographers.
	Example	To a certain degree, you might bring an implication of an ultimate happiness at present.
	Practice	
3	Phrase	There is rarely, if ever, ….
	Original Sentence.	There is rarely, if ever, a reminder that this person—this very same smiling person—is fragile enough to die.
	Example	There is rarely, if ever, anyone who luxuriates at a beach resort with the cash-the-cheque, and still construct enviable future.
	Practice	

4	Phrase	How can you reconcile …
	Original Sentence.	How can you reconcile social media's giddy artificiality with death's stone-cold reality?
	Example	How can you reconcile the ephemeral bacchanal with the compromised quality life in the future
	Practice	
5	Phrase	The more …the more …
	Original Sentence.	The more time you spend on Facebook, engaging with the social detritus of your friends, former friends, and hope-to-be friends, the more you sidestep the most central truth of your own existence.
	Example	The more we find unproductive enjoyment today, the less reliable future will come.
	Practice	
6	Phrase	… a more realistic suggestion revolves around
	Original Sentence.	But realizing that everyone, myself included, needs social media for practical life purposes, a more realistic suggestion revolves around mindfulness.
	Example	A more realistic suggestion to live healthy life in the future while enjoying the present always revolves around saving, preserving resources now to keep it warm.
	Practice	
7	Phrase	this may sound like an empty word, but I believe that
	Original Sentence.	"Mindfulness"—this may sound like an empty word, but I believe that it encapsulates the overarching message that I've tried to drive home throughout a semester of column writing.
	Example	This may sound like an empty word, but I value stability over the day-to-day enjoyment.
	Practice	

SAMPLE ESSAY 6

Essay Prompt

As you read the passage below, consider how Sabrina G. Lee uses

♦evidence, such as facts or examples, to support claims.

♦reasoning to develop ideas and to connect claims and evidence.

♦stylistic or persuasive elements, such as word choice or appeals to emotion, to add power to the ideas expressed.

Adopted from Sabrina G. Lee *"Denying climate change is not just wrong, it's dangerous"*

© February 20, 2009 The Crimson, Harvard University

Just when I was starting to get used to the passionate debates that characterize meals in Annenberg, a recent dinner conversation threw me a curveball. Last week, I had the unique—and frustrating—privilege of dining with the last individual on earth who does not believe in global warming.

Or so I thought. Further research indicates that my acquaintance was far from alone; according to a 2008 Gallup poll, about 11 percent of Americans still think that global warming "will never happen." (Within the scientific community, this statistic is only three percent.) Perhaps most disturbingly, the study reports that 13 percent of Americans believe that no further climate control measures are necessary—in other words, that we as a society should take no action to further reduce carbon emissions or attempt to combat global warming in any way.

Whether these "unbelievers" remain unconvinced due to differing interpretations of the data or mere apathy, their stance is not only untenable, but also dangerous. Though it's easy to brush off such wrongheaded beliefs in our relativistic culture, those who think global warming is a hoax are not simply another case of mere "difference of opinion." These people are gambling the welfare of the entire planet on the off-chance that the majority is wrong.

Evidence that the average temperature on Earth is rising is abundant and convincing, but I suspect I would be preaching to the converted if I were to summarize it here. The bottom line is that the scientific community has come to a clear consensus that the evidence of a warming trend is "unequivocal" and that human activity has "very likely" been the main cause for that change over the last 50 years. It is thus troubling that one in five Americans remain unconvinced by the vast majority of the scientific community that we have an immediate obligation to change our behavior and to protect our planet.

Beyond the scientific evidence, one can support a plan of action that reduces carbon emissions based on moral considerations alone. In an article entitled "Perspectives on Environmental Change: A Basis for Action," Professor Michael B. McElroy of Harvard's Center for Earth and Planetary Physics cites Pope John Paul II's opinion on global warming as he expressed it nearly 20 years ago: "Theology, philosophy and science all speak of a harmonious universe, of a cosmos endowed with its own integrity, its own internal, dynamic nature. This order must be respected. The human race is called to explore this order, to examine it with due care and to make use of it while safeguarding its integrity."

McElroy himself reflects that humans do not "have the right to place the balance of the global life support system at risk when there are sensible actions that can be taken to at least slow the pace of human-induced change." Put another way, the ethical imperative of preserving our planet outweighs the groundless opinions stubbornly maintained by a global warming skeptic.

This may seem pessimistic, but unfounded optimism is a privilege humanity cannot afford with only one planet to protect. Scientists have informed us of the imminent dangers of global warming, and we have the tools at hand to combat it. All that is needed now is a concerted, united effort to effect change. Those who deny the geological deterioration that is likely already underway are both foolish and disrespectful to future generations of our species and others. If preserving life on Earth as we know it is not reason enough to pay higher taxes, take public transportation, and err on the side of caution, I cannot imagine what else is.

Sample Essay 6 based on Reading / Analysis / Writing Scoring Rubric

	INTRODUCTION	
1 Thesis statement (topic sentence)	The article "Denying climate change is not just wrong, it's dangerous" written by Sabrina G. Lee makes an argument supporting that Global warming is a real imminent threat, and should be treated not only by scientific judgment but also by the ethical imperative.	
	(Title + the author's name + the central argument) ✓Demonstrates thorough comprehension of the source text ✓Shows an understanding of the text's central idea ✓Includes a skillful introduction	
2 Supporting detail	Sabrina's approach to her argument encompasses her personal anecdote, the polls from both regular American citizens and scientists, and a quotation from Harvard professor, and even one from the Pope.	
	✓Makes skillful use of textual evidence (quotations, paraphrases or both)	
3 Analysis of the thesis & supporting details	Within an ironic response from common folks is her connection to the argument that intensify our moral hazard and the ethical responsibility to this man-made climate change.	
	✓Offers an insightful analysis of the source text ✓Offers a well-considered evaluation of the author's use of evidence, reasoning, stylistic and persuasive elements	

BODY PARAGRAPH 1	
4 Contrasting point (topic sentence)	Sabrina starts her article off by recounting a recent encounter—"I had the unique—and frustrating—privilege of dining with the last individual on earth who does not believe in global warming".
	✓Includes a precise central claim. ✓Makes skillful use of textual evidence (quotations, paraphrases or both)
5 Supporting detail	She then immediately reminds her reader that she was wrong, "according to a 2008 Gallup poll, about 11 percent of Americans still think that global warming "will never happen.".
	✓Offers a thorough, well-considered evaluation of the author's use of persuasive elements, and/or feature(s) of the student's own choosing.
6 Analysis of the thesis & Supporting Details	Sabrina challenges her reader's emotion--instead of establishing her theory or argument according to a scientific data. She argues what is in people's mind about the issue she is about to elaborate. This strategy puts the reader into a bit uncomfortable position because not quite a few of us treat global warming as an imminent threat like losing jobs or sluggish economy. Once we admit we are within this 11 percent, we might feel guilty. In this sense, the author already fulfills her intention: garnering the reader's attention.
	✓Offers an insightful analysis of the source text and demonstrates a sophisticated understanding of the analytical task. ✓Offers a thorough, well-considered evaluation of the author's use of evidence, reasoning, and/or stylistic and persuasive elements, and/or feature(s) of the student's own choosing. ✓Contains relevant, sufficient, and strategically chosen support for claim(s) or point(s) made. ✓Focuses consistently on those features of the text that are most relevant to addressing the task.

BODY PARAGRAPH 2	
7 Central idea	By insinuating "that 13 percent of Americans believe that no further climate control measures are necessary", Sabrina warns the reader such a mindset of the unconvinced is "not only untenable, but also dangerous."
	✓ Shows an understanding of the text's central idea(s) and of most important details and how they interrelate, demonstrating a comprehensive understanding of the text.
8 Analysis of the thesis & supporting details	Sabrina continuously wishes to resort to the reader's emotion by touching their morals. I believe she elaborates her reasoning because an issue like global warming could be felt quite distanced or even cliché, not enough to intensify the reader's mental charge. I find that she utilizes words like "moral", "ethical", "conscious" a lot. There, she employs a quote from Pope John Paul II cited by Professor Michael B. McElroy of Harvard's Center for Earth and Planetary Physics: "Theology, philosophy and science all speak of a harmonious universe, of a cosmos endowed with its own integrity, its own internal, dynamic nature. This order must be respected." Her stylistic approach to the issue reflects and inspires the minds of the audience-- within those one-in-five unconvinced folks in America, who are accustomed to living with shadow of smog, but feel composure because of a simple denial. Sabrina understood that she can never erupt a guilty feeling from the reader— especially those who are global warming skeptics.
	✓ Offers a thorough, well-considered evaluation of the author's use of evidence, reasoning, and/or stylistic and persuasive elements, and/or feature(s) of the student's own choosing. ✓ Contains relevant, sufficient, and strategically chosen support for claim(s) or point (s) made. (Include - statistics- data- official names)

	BODY PARAGRAPH 3
9 Central Idea	In her final paragraph, she persuades the reader not to be " foolish and disrespectful to future generations of our species and others.".
	✓Includes a precise central claim.
10 Analysis of the thesis & supporting details	She artfully uses appeal to pathos to inform global warming is imminent danger. Throughout the article, she does not employs statistics or scientific data much. Understanding that global warming is a constant, unending, low-level threat to not a few Americans, she didn't not link the issue to a flamboyant numbers with a big word. She persuades her reader to be vigilant and reasonable. By doing so, Sabrina challenges the reader and addresses to be sanity and make good judgment.

	✓The response demonstrates a consistent use of precise word choice. The response
	    maintains a formal style and objective tone.
	✓Contains relevant, sufficient, and strategically chosen support for claim(s) or point(s)
	    made.

	CONCLUSION
11 Restatement of the central claim	Writing as a reaction to a unique person's rebuttal that global warming is hoax. Sabrina articulates her disappointment and how some people are illogical and nonchalant to the imminent threat to the earth. She argues that we must preserve the earth. She enlightens the reader by strategically employing her personal short story, insightful word choice, statistics, and a quote.
	✓Includes a skilful introduction and conclusion. ✓The response demonstrates a deliberate and highly effective progression of ideas both within paragraphs and throughout the essay.

Transitional Phrase Practice

Direction
Please read the transitional phrases and the example sentences below.
Using the same phrase, create your own sentence in the practice line.
Each sentence does not have to be related to each other.

Topic: People attend college or university for many different reasons (for example, new experiences, career preparation, increased knowledge). Why do you think people attend college or university?

1	Phrase	…is not only untenable, but also dangerous..
	Original Sentence.	Whether these "unbelievers" remain unconvinced due to differing interpretations of the data or mere apathy, their stance is not only untenable, but also dangerous.
	Example	As we are all investors of our future, expecting an awesome career without a college degree is not only untenable, but also dangerous.
	Practice	
2	Phrase	Evidence that … is abundant and convincing,
	Original Sentence.	Evidence that the average temperature on Earth is rising is abundant and convincing, but I suspect I would be preaching to the converted if I were to summarize it here.
	Example	Evidence that college degree will safeguard our future is abundant and convincing.
	Practice	
3	Phrase	The bottom line is that …
	Original Sentence.	The bottom line is that the scientific community has come to a clear consensus that the evidence of a warming trend is "unequivocal" and that human activity has "very likely" been the main cause for that change over the last 50 years.
	Example	The bottom line is that--given the risks of becoming a high debtor by the time you graduate due to the mounting college loan—you should consider technical school.
	Practice	

4	Phrase	Put another way, …
	Original Sentence.	Put another way, the ethical imperative of preserving our planet outweighs the groundless opinions stubbornly maintained by a global warming skeptic.
	Example	Put another way, the amount of tuition paid each year in college will be the working capital in your career after graduation.
	Practice	
5	Phrase	This may seem pessimistic, but unfounded optimism …
	Original Sentence.	This may seem pessimistic, but unfounded optimism is a privilege humanity cannot afford with only one planet to protect.
	Example	This may seem pessimistic at first by simply looking at the projected debts you are supposed to owe for tuition and living expenses while attending university, but unfounded optimism that you could get a nice job without a college degree will be even more disturbing anticipation.
	Practice	
6	Phrase	All that is needed now is…
	Original Sentence.	All that is needed now is a concerted, united effort to effect change.
	Example	There might still be disputes—especially about exorbitant costs of tuition— but all that is needed now is education and training.
	Practice	

Ch. 1

Ch. 2

Ch. 3

Ch. 4

Ch. 5

Ch. 6

Ch. 7

Ch. 8

Ch. 9

Ch. 10

SAMPLE ESSAY 7

Essay Prompt

As you read the passage below, consider how Marshall Zhang uses

♦evidence, such as facts or examples, to support claims.

♦reasoning to develop ideas and to connect claims and evidence.
♦stylistic or persuasive elements, such as word choice or appeals to emotion, to add power to the ideas expressed.

Adopted from Marshall Zhang *"The Happiness Sale"*
© February 20, 2016 The Crimson, Harvard University

A. J. Maxwell's was an archetypal New York steakhouse on the corner of 48th and 6th in the heart of midtown Manhattan. There, a few weeks after my middle school graduation, my family splurged on a celebration of our first road trip to America. I distinctly remember the forty-dollar entrées that dotted the menu (the opulence of it all!), and sinking my teeth into a steak that the Old Spaghetti Factories I was used to could only dream of serving.

Today, A. J. Maxwell's is closed after years of poor reviews, with references to overpriced food and jerky-like steaks dating back to far before my visit. Though I can't say for certain, I suspect the steak I had eight years ago was not, in any particular way, noteworthy in the grand scheme of beef. But somehow that steak remains in my mind, more vividly than any steak I've had since, as close to perfection as a slab of meat can be.

Diminishing marginal utility is one way to understand this seeming contradiction. Loosely, this is the idea that the marginal (read: additional) utility (read: benefit) of extra stuff diminishes as we have more stuff to begin with: We would love an extra dollar if we only had ten dollars to our names, but could probably care less about the same dollar as millionaires. For similar reasons, my very first fancy steak—though not incredible per se—was far more memorable than my tenth. The first let me peek into a whole new world of fine dining, while the tenth probably wasn't all that special next to the nine other fancy steaks before it.

As thoroughly broke college students who in the median will earn between $50,000 and $69,999 upon graduation and likely even more later in life, our marginal utility is high now relative to our expected marginal utility 20 years down the road. In other words, as we become older and richer, things and experiences that amaze us now will probably lose their luster.

We might understand this as a sale on happiness: Today, it would almost certainly take more than forty dollars to buy a steak as incredible to me as the one my 13-year-old self savored so dearly at A. J. Maxwell's.

In more concrete terms, imagine we knew that, like the average American, we would be spending $55,000 every year by the middle of our lives (note, for the record, that the argument here works even if we're not planning on being a big future spender). If we had the power to move a thousand dollars of that spending to today, we almost certainly would. Imagine if we had an extra grand today! Instead of a trip into Boston, we could take a once-in-a-lifetime trip to Paris; instead of celebrating semester-end with instant noodles, we could treat our best friends to dinner at the city's finest restaurant. On a smaller scale, instead of brain break, we could satiate a late-night Kong craving as soon as it materialized without guilt (at least of the monetary kind). Cheap Chinese food hits the spot in a way only college students can truly appreciate: There is a reason—diminishing marginal utility—our parents don't like the Kong as much as we do. And we could do all of this in exchange for the negligible sacrifice of consuming $54,000 instead of $55,000 worth of stuff over one year, many years from now.

Even Macklemore couldn't find a better deal.

It turns out that financial markets have created a way for us to move money through time in exactly this way: debt. We can borrow money from the bank today and pay it back with our higher incomes in the future, effectively taking out a loan from our richer, future self. The logic of introductory economics would say that we should squeeze every last penny out of the happiness sale in this way, borrowing

large amounts of money to finance increased spending today until we could expect to consume roughly the same amount at every point in our lifetimes.

But perfectly spreading out our consumption like this is impossible in practice and probably undesirable to boot. Few banks would be willing to issue the large loans we would need, and we might be worried about the risk of being saddled with debt if we ended up earning less than we expected to. Furthermore, consumption is often positional, in the sense that what matters isn't necessarily how much we consume, but how much we consume relative to those around us. In other words, your 20-year class reunion might not be a lot of fun if you're paying down debt while your classmates are busy buying nice houses.

On the other hand, it is easy to veer too far in the opposite direction. We've been taught since childhood to spend when we know we'll have more and save precisely when we have little. <u>Though this seems fairly reasonable, it certainly doesn't sound right to teach farmers to gorge themselves during good harvests and only attempt to store grain in bad harvests.</u> Rather, they should be saving excess grain in good years so that they have more to eat in bad years. <u>While a perfectly smoothed consumption profile is non-optimal, there is no reason to believe that the extremely jagged consumption pattern that we naturally fall into is any better.</u> The sweet spot is likely somewhere in between; hence, spending a little more today than we otherwise unreflectively might and buying marginal utility on clearance should move us closer to where we optimally ought to be.

This is not an argument for financial profligacy. Taking out a loan for $10,000 against our future income to buy a new Hermès purse today is probably a bad idea. Spending for the sake of spending isn't likely to make us substantially more content with our lives. But there will likely never be another time in our lives when happiness today can be found for so cheap relative to happiness tomorrow. From the crab rangoons that we've been craving all night to the unforgettable college adventure abroad we've always wanted to take, life's sale on happiness awaits.

Sample Essay 7 based on Reading / Analysis / Writing Scoring Rubric

Ch. 1

Ch. 2

Ch. 3

Ch. 4

Ch. 5

Ch. 6

Ch. 7

Ch. 8

Ch. 9

Ch. 10

	INTRODUCTION
1 Thesis statement (topic sentence)	In his article " The Happiness Sale", the author Marshall Zhang searches for happiness—a theme per se more often than not quite complex and therefore requires metaphysical approach—in very unique but still very affordable way that no other person has gone (bought) before.
	✓(Title + the author's name + the central argument) ✓ Demonstrates thorough comprehension of the source text ✓Shows an understanding of the text's central idea ✓Includes a skilful introduction
2 Supporting detail	He starts his argument with his personal anecdote he experienced, then further elaborates his perspective through economic theory, and finally how financial markets practically utilize his theory, and finally the limitation of his theory from the view of positional relativity.
	✓Makes skilful use of textual evidence (quotations, paraphrases or both)
3 Analysis of the thesis & supporting details	His reasoning through real-life experience and insightful analysis of his brainchild theory convincingly appeals to the reader.
	✓Offers an insightful analysis of the source text ✓Offers a well-considered evaluation of the author's use of evidence, reasoning, stylistic and persuasive elements.

BODY PARAGRAPH 1	
4 Contrasting point (topic sentence)	Marshall's insightful approach to his analysis--relocating the fraction of future earnings into the present in order to realize and optimize immediate happiness starts with his personal anecdote, in which he invites his audience to A.J Maxwell steakhouse where he had his first steak 8 years ago.
	✓Includes a precise central claim. ✓Makes skillful use of textual evidence (quotations, paraphrases or both)
5 Supporting detail	He connects to the reader with a vivid recollection of his very first steak he ever had in his life. Soon after, Marshall debunks the truth with nothing but irony that "A.J. Maxwell's is closed after years of poor reviews, overpriced food and jerky-like steaks…."
	✓Offers a thorough, well-considered evaluation of the author's use of persuasive elements, and/or feature(s) of the student's own choosing.
6 Analysis of the thesis & supporting details	There begins his theory "marginal utility". Marshall explains the seeming contradiction he experienced at A.J. Maxwell: why we are surprised no more with the identical quality of steak; why it requires a lot more money at present to experience the same amazement we had in the past. What makes Marshall's theory unique and enthralling to the reader is that his theory is not embedded on economics, but instead it aptly and lightly wharfs on our mental psychic. Rather than inculcating his reader with figures in economic theory, he suggests a singular way to materialize happiness by saying "our marginal utility is high now relative to our expected marginal utility 20 years down the road. " "As we become older and richer, things and experiences that amaze us now will probably lose their luster. We might understand this as a sale on happiness."

HARVARD STUDENT ESSAY ANALAYS

Ch. 1

Ch. 2

Ch. 3

Ch. 4

Ch. 5

Ch. 6

Ch. 7

Ch. 8

Ch. 9

Ch. 10

6 Analysis of the thesis & supporting details	✓Offers an insightful analysis of the source text and demonstrates a sophisticated understanding of the analytical task. ✓Offers a thorough, well-considered evaluation of the author's use of evidence, reasoning, and/or stylistic and persuasive elements, and/or feature(s) of the student's own choosing. ✓Contains relevant, sufficient, and strategically chosen support for claim(s) or point (s) made. ✓Focuses consistently on those features of the text that are most relevant to addressing the task.

BODY PARAGRAPH 2

7 Central idea	Marshall's hypothesis prominently turns its head to the real market. "It turns out that financial markets have created a way for us to move money through time in exactly this way: debt."
	✓Shows an understanding of the text's central idea(s) and of most important details and how they interrelate, demonstrating a comprehensive understanding of the text.
8 Analysis of the thesis & supporting details	Marshall enlightens the reader how his theory " marginal utility" actually functions in reality by analogously exemplifying bank loan. He explains we can borrow money from bank or bank lend money to consumers today, expecting higher income can be realized in the future. His bank loan analogy effectively introduces the reader how his theory is functioning that allows us to enjoy happiness throughout time. His article is insightful—especially to those who live with a fixed budget in their daily basis. The reader will admit that his article can actually improve the value of some of our lives, at least in theory.
	✓Offers a thorough, well-considered evaluation of the author's use of evidence, reasoning, and/or stylistic and persuasive elements, and/or feature(s) of the student's own choosing. ✓Contains relevant, sufficient, and strategically chosen support for claim(s) or point (s) made. (Include - statistics- data- official names)

BODY PARAGRAPH 3	
9 Central Idea	Finally, to solidify his argument, Marshall illustrates a view of an old parable that we should spend more when we have more, and save when we have little. He insightfully and yet paradoxically argues against it. "farmers to gorge during good harvests and only attempt to store grain in bad harvests." Here, he suggests more accessible and less expensive way of buying happiness from the up-side-down point of view on old saying.
	✓Includes a precise central claim.
10 Analysis of the thesis & supporting details	However, Marshall warns the reader to be able to distinguish his hypothesis from profligacy. He points out that his theory is based on searching for happiness today that never will likely be found in another time future in our lives—at a relatively cheaper price. To qualify his argument, he introduces a positional consumption theory. That is, the way we feel happiness is comparative and what matters is how we feel about the present satisfaction compared to others. His college reunion analogy expresses clearly about the limitation and interpretational chasm in his hypothesis.
	✓The response demonstrates a consistent use of precise word choice. The response maintains a formal style and objective tone. ✓Contains relevant, sufficient, and strategically chosen support for claim(s) or point (s) made.
CONCLUSION	
11 Restatement of the central claim	Throughout the article, Marshall insightfully articulates the basis of his hypothesis, using vivid personal anecdote, analogy, and brilliant logic underpinning his analysis. His writing is persuasive and appeals to the reader not because it is based on statistics or grand economic theory, but because it is a revision of our mindset that can teach the reader to find happiness at present at an affordable way.
	✓Includes a skillful introduction and conclusion. ✓The response demonstrates a deliberate and highly effective progression of ideas both within paragraphs and throughout the essay.

Transitional Phrase Practice

Direction
Please read the transitional phrases and the example sentences below.
Using the same phrase, create your own sentence in the practice line.
Each sentence does not have to be related to each other.

Topic: "When people succeed, it is because of hard work. Luck has nothing to do with success."

1	Phrase	It turns out that …
	Original Sentence.	It turns out that financial markets have created a way for us to move money through time in exactly this way: debt.
	Example	Each time I meet a socially or financially successful individual, it turns out that the person is not at all any different from other common folks—not shrouded by incredible luck or talents.
	Practice	
2	Phrase	But … is impossible in practice and probably undesirable to …
	Original Sentence.	But perfectly spreading out our consumption like this is impossible in practice and probably undesirable to boot.
	Example	Imitating successful people's life styles is impossible in practice and probably undesirable.
	Practice	
3	Phrase	Furthermore, … is often positional, in the sense that …
	Original Sentence.	Furthermore, consumption is often positional, in the sense that what matters isn't necessarily how much we consume, but how much we consume relative to those around us.
	Example	Furthermore, lumping all the rich people's characters together—superficially—is nothing more than as if a girl sprays on all the samples from the perfumery counter
	Practice	

Ch. 3

Ch. 4

Ch. 5

Ch. 6

Ch. 7

Ch. 8

Ch. 9

Ch. 10

4	Phrase	Though this seems fairly reasonable,... it certainly doesn't sound right
	Original Sentence.	Though this seems fairly reasonable, it certainly doesn't sound right to teach farmers to gorge themselves during good harvests and only attempt to store grain in bad harvests.
	Example	Though imitating a financial wizard's life style and idea seems fairly ideal, It doesn't sound right to obey whatever s/he does just because of she is rich.
	Practice	
5	Phrase	There is no reason to believe that...
	Original Sentence.	While a perfectly smoothed consumption profile is non-optimal, there is no reason to believe that the extremely jagged consumption pattern that we naturally fall into is any better.
	Example	There is no doubt that either hard work or luck definitely contributes one's success, there is no also reason to believe one has to be smart to bring both luck and hard work.
	Practice	
6	Phrase	The sweet spot is likely somewhere in between; hence, ...than we otherwise unreflectively might
	Original Sentence.	The sweet spot is likely somewhere in between; hence, spending a little more today than we otherwise unreflectively might and buying marginal utility on clearance should move us closer to where we optimally ought to be.
	Example	The sweet spot is likely finding the goldilocks; hence, knowing the best of you and fashioning it rather than unreflectively copying richer people should move us closer to success.
	Practice	

Ch. 1

Ch. 2

Ch. 3

Ch. 4

Ch. 5

Ch. 6

Ch. 7

Ch. 8

Ch. 9

Ch. 10

SAMPLE ESSAY 8

Essay Prompt

As you read the passage below, consider how Deeclan P. Garvey uses

♦evidence, such as facts or examples, to support claims.

♦reasoning to develop ideas and to connect claims and evidence.
♦stylistic or persuasive elements, such as word choice or appeals to emotion, to add power to the ideas expressed.

Adopted from "Virtual Reality But Real Consequences"
© April 18, 2014The Crimson, Harvard University

More than usual, these past few weeks in the United States have been a time of sheer idiocy. A woman tried to throw a shoe at former Secretary of State Hillary Rodham Clinton. Some moron placed a fake bomb at the finish line of the Boston Marathon. Bubba Watson ate at a Waffle House. But the pièce-de-résistance of this festival of stupidity must have been Twitter user @QueenDemetriax_'s contribution. On Sunday morning she tweeted the following to the American Airlines corporate account:

American Airlines corporate account:
SARAH@QUEENDEMETRIZX. @AMFERICANAIR
HELLOW MY NAME'S IBRAHIM AND I'M FROM AFGHANISTAN. I'M PART OF AL QAIDA AND ON JUNE 1ST I'M GONNA DO SOMETHING REALLY BIG BYE. 10:37 AM – 13 APR 2014

Within minutes, the company responded:
@QUEENDEMETRIAX_ SARAH, WE TAKE THESE THREATS VERY SERIOUSLY. YOUR IP ADDRESS AND DETAILS WILL BE FORWARDED TO SECURITY AND THE FBI. COURTESY OF TWITTER

Despite her frantic claims that she was "kidding," Dutch officials showed up at the Rotterdam native's house and arrested her on the spot, drawing to a close a news story that would have been completely fruitless had it not provided me a topic to write about. For that, you and I both have @QueenDemetriax_'s unreliable frontal lobe to thank.

What this narrative seems to highlight however is not merely one girl's lapse in judgment (especially considering dozens of teenagers followed her lead), but a larger phenomenon in which Internet users fail to associate their online actions with real-world consequences. Senseless and shortsighted uses of the Internet have led to unemployment, pedophilia, robberies, political scandals, and arrests.

Back when my family didn't take trips without me, I always used to tease my dad for telling my siblings and I not to post pictures on vacation because "you don't know who's going to see that we aren't at home." You were right, and I'm sorry (this realization has become a trend now that I'm in college).

Older generations have always entertained a slight distrust of new technologies, fearing the limits of their privacy. And their kids have always gotten entertainment from that distrust. "No Grandpa, Gmail isn't asking for your birthday so they can steal your pension." "Yes, Mom, that's a webcam. No, Mom, the government can't watch you through it." Although…

But all kidding aside, maybe more Internet users need figures like my dad reminding them that there is in fact a world that exists beyond the perimeters of their various screens. <u>One of the defining characteristics of our generation is our increasing technological proficiency and ability to master new platforms so quickly.</u> <u>But we've grown so accustomed to computers and social media that the magnitude of our online actions is forgotten.</u> Despite what some privacy settings may claim, anything posted online is available to anyone at any time.

The Internet allows some to believe they can cleanly divorce their online persona with their day-to-day life. In social media's early days, such a split might have been feasible. But today everyone and his mother (including my own) is on Twitter, Facebook, Instagram, and Vine (yep, she's on all of them), and your account is merely an extension of your identity. "What I do online is my own business" or "It was only Twitter" no longer constitute valid excuses—to the public, your employer, your significant other, or anyone else. The novelty of these websites and applications has worn off, and for all intents and purposes, online postings are just as legitimate a form of communication as human interaction.

Academics who study human behavior and the brain are just now beginning to understand the cognitive impact of social media on its 1.73 billion users worldwide. Significant levels of Internet usage can lead to loneliness, jealousy, suicidality, and memory deficiency. But the most fundamental change wrought by the Internet is our unprecedented need for constant and immediate affirmation. I'll be the first to admit, the number of likes I receive on a post has a direct impact on my mood in the short-run. After accumulating 18 favorites on some stupid tweet over winter break, I spent the rest of the day parading around my house like a king.

<u>For those of you who dismiss the significance of this effect, I'll leave you with this.</u> What else could have possibly motivated @QueenDemetriax_ to hit the send button? Was she testing American Airlines's security procedures? Is she actually the worst terrorist of all time? No, and I don't think so.

Sample Essay 8 based on Reading / Analysis / Writing Scoring Rubric

Ch. 1

Ch. 2

Ch. 3

Ch. 4

Ch. 5

Ch. 6

Ch. 7

Ch. 8

Ch. 9

Ch. 10

	INTRODUCTION
1	In the article, "Virtual Reality But Real Consequences", the author by Declan P. Garvey warns a significant consequence that can cause to the mindless SNS users.
Thesis statement (topic sentence)	✓(Title + the author's name + the central argument) ✓Demonstrates thorough comprehension of the source text ✓Shows an understanding of the text's central idea ✓Includes a skillful introduction
2 Analysis of the thesis & supporting details	Strategies Declan employs to support his argument revolve around one recent incidence that he further generalizes and gives a cautious advice to the internet users. Although he rarely relies on statistical data and some meaningful quotation to back up his analysis, Decaln's message to the reader penetrates promptly with carefully selected word choices and the utilization of stylistic devices such as rhetorical question, juxtaposition, and paradox. As his primary audience would be the young generation who spend significant time on SNS and value it as a most pivotal communication tool, Declan's quintessential example that used an example of a young reckless tweeter user and the narrative skills to deliver his message build enough foundation to earn approval of his view.
	✓Offers an insightful analysis of the source text ✓Offers a well-considered evaluation of the author's use of evidence, reasoning, stylistic and persuasive elements.
	BODY PARAGRAPH 1
3 Contrasting point (topic sentence)	In his introduction paragraph, Decaln starts with some of the recent idiosyncratic behaviors of young people, and then moves quickly to his theme, "QueenDemetriax's bomb threat via Tweet, rewarding it as the piece-de-resistance of stupidity.

3 Contrasting point	✓ Includes a precise central claim. ✓ Makes skillful use of textual evidence (quotations, paraphrases or both)
4 Analysis of the thesis & supporting details	The issue seemingly starting as a warning against some irresponsible youth, who threatens the national security, in fact, aims at broader audience. Different from humorous introduction, his article takes control of the debate with carefully measured word choices like "a larger phenomenon in which Internet users fail to associate their online actions with real-world consequences." He focuses that the gravity of irresponsible actions in virtual reality is solely the problem of individual and this problem only intensifies these days.
	✓ Offers an insightful analysis of the source text and demonstrates a sophisticated understanding of the analytical task. ✓ Offers a thorough, well-considered evaluation of the author's use of evidence, reasoning, and/or stylistic and persuasive elements, and/or feature(s) of the student's own choosing. ✓ Contains relevant, sufficient, and strategically chosen support for claim(s) or point (s) made. ✓ Focuses consistently on those features of the text that are most relevant to address-

BODY PARAGRAPH 2

5 Central idea	To support his argument, Decaln uses a kind of familiar juxtaposition: how older generation like his father, grandpa, and mom were extremely cautious—or excessively suspicious--about using internet.
	✓ Shows an understanding of the text's central idea(s) and of most important details and how they interrelate, demonstrating a comprehensive understanding of the text.

6 Analysis of the thesis & supporting details	Underpinning this seemingly humorous personal family story lies a stark contrast between the view of older generation and the levity of young generation's internet use. His stylistic approach cuts a possible doubt and bolsters his presentation. In describing dexterous skills of modern youth and its consequence, Decaln uses paradox again. "But we've grown so accustomed to computers and social media that the magnitude of our online actions is forgotten." Decaln inculcates the reader how adversely and inevitably our technological adeptness recreated a dumb and morally hazardous world. From the acute eyes of youth, older generation who can't do anything with computer might look helpless. This is almost a solid fact that emphasizes the author's point in exactly opposite way. That youth are so adept in their computer and technological gadgets, they find no true value or significance of communication they post online.
	✓ Offers a thorough, well-considered evaluation of the author's use of evidence, reasoning, and/or stylistic and persuasive elements, and/or feature(s) of the student's own choosing. ✓ Contains relevant, sufficient, and strategically chosen support for claim(s) or point(s) made. (Include - statistics- data- official names)

Ch. 1
Ch. 2
Ch. 3
Ch. 4
Ch. 5
Ch. 6
Ch. 7
Ch. 8
Ch. 9
Ch. 10

	CONCLUSION
7 Restatement of the central claim	Overall, Decaln's argument is strong in that the usage of an insightful example, effort to assimilate with the audience by introducing a generally accepted old generation's overreaction to the internet, and retrospection himself as an avid SNS user, an attempt to be equal to the audience. Problems of SNS and internet has been a hotly debated issue with no clear consensus. We all know the price we should pay for not using or using the internet. Decaln tries to find a goldilocks that the reader can jump into the safe spot for general agreement. His stylistic devices like rhetorical questions, paradox, anecdote accomplish the purpose to bring the audience's response.
	✓Includes a skillful introduction and conclusion. ✓The response demonstrates a deliberate and highly effective progression of ideas both within paragraphs and throughout the essay.

Transitional Phrase Practice

Direction

Please read the transitional phrases and the example sentences below.
Using the same phrase, create your own sentence in the practice line.
Each sentence does not have to be related to each other.

Topic: Some people believe that the Earth is being harmed by human activity. Others feel that human activity makes the Earth a better place to live. What is your opinion?

1	Phrase	the pièce-de-résistance ....
	Original Sentence.	But the pièce-de-résistance of this festival of stupidity must have been Twitter user @QueenDemetriax_'s contribution.
	Example	The piece-de-resistance of those who still scoff at the global warming should visit Florida experiencing a dry flooding.
	Practice	
2	Phrase	INVERSION IN 'IF CLAUSE'
	Original Sentence.	a news story that would have been completely fruitless had it not provided me a topic to write about.
	Example	The statistics shows that approximately every $ 8 would have been saved on our economy had we spent every $1 on a environmental protection program.
	Practice	
3	Phrase	What this narrative seems to highlight, however, is not merely ... but a larger phenomenon in which...
	Original Sentence.	What this narrative seems to highlight however is not merely one girl's lapse in judgment (especially considering dozens of teenagers followed her lead), but a larger phenomenon in which Internet users fail to associate their online actions with real-world consequences.
	Example	What this narrative seems to highlight, however, is not merely recasting the incidence of oil spill in pacific ocean, but a larger phenomenon in which many high rank government officials now were used to be the officials in charge during the incidence in 1990 that we demand clarification.
	Practice	

Ch. 1

Ch. 2

Ch. 3

Ch. 4

Ch. 5

Ch. 6

Ch. 7

Ch. 8

Ch. 9

Ch. 10

4	Phrase	One of the defining characteristics ….
	Original Sentence.	One of the defining characteristics of our generation is our increasing technological proficiency and ability to master new platforms so quickly.
	Example	One of the defining characteristics of developing countries for being accused of the world-pollution-manufacturers is the widespread impunity to the pollution related crimes.
	Practice	
5	Phrase	SO ~ THAT CLAUSE
	Original Sentence.	But we've grown so accustomed to computers and social media that the magnitude of our online actions is forgotten.
	Example	Such a widespread impunity will ensure another and bigger pollution crime so complexly organized and massive in operation that it will be impossible to stop polluting the environment
	Practice	
6	Phrase	For those of you who dismiss the significance of this effect, I'll leave you with this.
	Original Sentence.	For those of you who dismiss the significance of this effect, I'll leave you with this.
	Example	For those of you who dismiss the significance of climate change, I'll leave you with this: By 2060, the entire east coast cities in U.S. will be submerged under the sea.
	Practice	

Ch. 1

 Ch. 2

 Ch. 3

 Ch. 4

 Ch. 5

 Ch. 6

 Ch. 7

 Ch. 8

 Ch. 9

 Ch. 10

SAMPLE ESSAY 9

Essay Prompt

As you read the passage below, consider how THE HARVARD CRIMSON STAFF uses

- ♦ evidence, such as facts or examples, to support claims.
- ♦ reasoning to develop ideas and to connect claims and evidence.
- ♦ stylistic or persuasive elements, such as word choice or appeals to emotion, to add power to the ideas expressed.

Adopted from THE HARVARD CRIMSON STAFF
"Standardized testing may be flawed, but it is unavoidable
" © October 3, 2007 The Crimson, Harvard University

When it comes to the standardized college admissions tests like the SAT and ACT, there's a lot to gripe about. Beyond bringing additional stress to the admissions process, it is unclear that standardized tests are really fair or measure actual aptitude. Indeed, studies have shown that standardized test scores are less effective than things like high school grades at predicting academic performance in college, are correlated with the socioeconomic status of test takers, and are subject to the influence of coaching and private tutoring, luxuries only available to those who can afford them.

Despite their many flaws, however, standardized tests are a necessary convenience for many schools, serving as a coarse method of comparison between the tens of thousands of applicants a school may consider every year. Steps should be taken to ameliorate the importance of these tests, but getting rid of them is unfortunately not a viable option.

The good news is that debate about the importance of standardized testing in college admissions finally seems to be spreading to those with the power to reform the system. Indeed, at the National Association for College Admissions Counseling (NACAC) Conference held last week, discussion about the importance of standardized testing took the limelight. And NACAC is taking action—it formed a Commission on the Use of Standardized Tests in Undergraduate Admission, chaired by Harvard Dean of Admissions William R. Fitzsimmons '67, which will issue a report next year.

The Commission's report is expected to address the effect of test preparation on student performance, test biases, and the possible advantages of using subject tests over the SAT. In addition, the Commission will also propose recommendations to college admissions officers and high school counselors on how they should view standardized tests, in light of the tests' potential weaknesses. These efforts are commendable, because identifying where the SAT falls short will not only increase admissions officers' awareness of the test's limitations, but also encourage the development of more reliable and more equitable methods of evaluation.

In the current admissions system, however, standardized tests will continue to serve a useful role for many colleges. Scores, although limited in their predictive power, still provide a nationally standardized benchmark against which admissions officers may quickly garner a rough idea of an applicant's comparative academic ability. As long as admissions committees are aware of the test's limitations and interpret scores with the applicant's socioeconomic background in mind, considering test scores may greatly expedite what would otherwise be an unmanageably complex admissions process.

To be sure, in an ideal world, colleges would not have to rely on scores at all when evaluating applicants. This is a luxury Harvard has—the College has a large admissions committee that is able to read every piece of paper that it receives. At Harvard, standardized tests are merely one additional indicator, not the difference between an acceptance letter and a rejection. This type of system is the ideal toward which all universities should strive.
Unfortunately, many schools do not have the resources to implement such a costly holistic evaluation process, especially large state schools.

For instance, the University of California at Los Angeles received upwards of 50,000 applications last year. Standardized tests might be a terrible system, but they are better than the alternatives.

What reformers and Fitzsimmons' Commission should focus on, then, is not getting rid of standardized tests but finding ways to level the playing field within the context of the existing system.
There are many ways to do so. The College Board, which administers the SAT, could reduce the cost of their expensive and lucrative test prep materials so that preparation becomes less of a luxury good.

Moreover, colleges could share with each other information on the quality of instruction of different high schools, making it easier for deluged admissions offices to judge a student's coursework relative to standards of his or her school.

In the long run, this would allow colleges to de-emphasize standardized testing and focus on other measures of aptitude. Such solutions would reduce the inequities imposed by standardized tests without destroying a useful tool because it is flawed.

As long as admissions committees are aware of the test's limitations and interpret scores with the applicant's socioeconomic background in mind, considering test scores may greatly expedite what would otherwise be an unmanageably complex admissions process.

Sample Essay 9 based on Reading / Analysis / Writing Scoring Rubric

	INTRODUCTION
1 Thesis statement (topic sentence)	<u>In the article</u> "Standardized testing may be flawed, but it is unavoidable" an editorial for the Harvard crimson, <u>the author argues that</u> standardized tests, although far from impeccable, serve their own purpose.
	(Title + the author's name + the central argument) ✓Demonstrates thorough comprehension of the source text ✓Shows an understanding of the text's central idea ✓Includes a skillful introduction
2 Supporting detail	<u>He believes</u> they would do more good than harm—<u>"a necessary convenience for many schools, serving as a coarse method of comparison"</u>.
	✓Makes skillful use of textual evidence (quotations, paraphrases or both)
3 Analysis of the thesis & supporting Details	<u>After reading this piece the reader will consent to the author's argument</u> not only because <u>his argument cements the core value of</u> the standardized testing, but also because, <u>like many other good writers who effectively plead with the audience to take his side, he employs reasoning based on persuasion, statistics, and a quote from established figures and organs. In that sense, this article demonstrates many analytical skills.</u>
	✓Offers an insightful analysis of the source text ✓Offers a well-considered evaluation of the author's use of evidence, reasoning, stylistic and persuasive elements.

	BODY PARAGRAPH 1
4 Contrasting point (topic sentence)	"When it comes to the standardized college admissions tests…there's a lot to gripe about."
	✓Includes a precise central claim. ✓Makes skillful use of textual evidence (quotations, paraphrases or both)
5 Supporting detail	The author ventures his revelation of the irrational aspects of the tests by conceding possible opponents' concern to the standardized tests, only later to reject it.
	✓Offers a thorough, well-considered evaluation of the author's use of persuasive elements, and/or feature(s) of the student's own choosing.
6 Analysis of the thesis & supporting details	Contrasting point is often viewed as a powerful leverage to bolster the author's argument. By presenting relatively reasonable opposing views, the author can inflate his tone and articulate the logic behind his reasoning. This approach is effective in that, throughout the article, not only does the author stratify the inevitable deficiencies of the current testing system, in which the author wishes to find a solution, but also offers alternatives to ameliorate the importance of the tests. He introduces those with power to reform the system such as the fact that the national Association for College Admissions Counselling had a conference, taking action to form a commission. He uses both reasoning and emotional appeal, backed by reliable sources, to penetrate the reader's neutral mind. He judiciously builds up his argument with block-by-block precision and top-to-bottom solution, initiating from the commission's report to advisory to high counselor about the tests.

Ch. 1   Ch. 2   Ch. 3   Ch. 4   Ch. 5   Ch. 6   Ch. 7   Ch. 8   Ch. 9   Ch. 10

Analysis of the thesis & supporting details	✓Offers an insightful analysis of the source text and demonstrates a sophisticated understanding of the analytical task. ✓Offers a thorough, well-considered evaluation of the author's use of evidence, reasoning, and/or stylistic and persuasive elements, and/or feature(s) of the student's own choosing. ✓Contains relevant, sufficient, and strategically chosen support for claim(s) or point(s) made. ✓Focuses consistently on those features of the text that are most relevant to addressing the task.
BODY PARAGRAPH 2	
7 Central idea	Additionally, the author appeals to the impracticality and infeasibility to getting rid of the standardized testing.
	✓Shows an understanding of the text's central idea(s) and of most important details and how they interrelate, demonstrating a comprehensive understanding of the
8 Supporting detail	He persuades the reader "that many schools do not have the resources to implement such a costly holistic evaluation process, especially large state schools." , should the current standardized tests be abolished. With a key phrase like "The University of California at Los Angeles received upwards of 50,000 applications last year."
	✓Makes skillful use of textual evidence (quotations, paraphrases, or both), demonstrating a complete understanding of the source text.

9 Analysis of the thesis & supporting details	Using this clear fact alone the author can reassure the reader that the current standardized testing system, under which universities measure applicants' scholastic aptitude, is not the best, but inevitable necessity. The figures like this with solid example such as the number of applicants UCLA receives every year clarifies that there are no better alternatives to replace the current testing system to evaluate every single applicants. By substantiating the numeric figures , the author expect that the reader will find very difficult to raise any, if there is, possible objections along, not to mention a better solution. The author achieves his goal by qualifying, categorizing, and acknowledging the deficiencies of the current system first. His strategic approach—instead of utilizing a black-and-white theory, a silver bullet, or panacea for unanimous—easily circumvents unfavorable issues, while proposing a blueprint for amelioration.
	✓Offers a thorough, well-considered evaluation of the author's use of evidence, reasoning, and/or stylistic and persuasive elements, and/or feature(s) of the student's own choosing. ✓Contains relevant, sufficient, and strategically chosen support for claim(s) or point(s) made. (Include - statistics- data- official names)

BODY PARAGRAPH 3	
10 Central Idea	An article focusing on whether to abolish standardized tests that have full of defects is not fairly clear-cut issue, but by carefully selecting diction (i.e. insinuating a utopian world), the author creates a strong juxtaposition.
	✓Includes a precise central claim.
11 Supporting detail	It is with word choice such as "To be sure, in an ideal world colleges would not have to rely on scores at all when evaluating applicants".
	✓Makes skillful use of textual evidence (quotations, paraphrases, or both), demonstrating a complete understanding of the source text.

12 Analysis of the thesis & supporting details	<u>Because the issue at hand is to</u> defend the system with full of problems, the author's main strategy is not to support the current system, <u>but rather</u> focuses on searching for possibilities to improve the system. <u>Some of the words choice the author used,</u> "but finding ways to level the playing field…", , "colleges could share with each other information…", <u>reveals how he want to communicate with and persuade the reader looking at the issue from the opposite angle. All of these statements display tone of persuasion, strategic selection, surely helping the author to imbue his message.</u>
	✓The response demonstrates a consistent use of precise word choice. The response maintains a formal style and objective tone. ✓Contains relevant, sufficient, and strategically chosen support for claim(s) or point(s) made.

CONCLUSION

13 Restatement of the central claim	<u>To sum up, it is through concession</u> that the author sells his argument. Qualified assessment of the current testing system, the disclosure of test's limited functionality and availability, out of which finding a concession as well as ways to ameliorate the system, all contribute to an exceptionally well-written argument. It is his utilization of these practices and more that make this article worthy of recognition. Upon finish reading his article, the reader will be nodding along in accordance with the author.
	✓Includes a skillful introduction and conclusion. ✓The response demonstrates a deliberate and highly effective progression of ideas both within paragraphs and throughout the essay.

Transitional Phrase Practice

Direction

Please read the transitional phrases and the example sentences below.
Using the same phrase, create your own sentence in the practice line.
Each sentence does not have to be related each other.
Prompt: What is the major qualification to be the best teacher?

Ch. 1
Ch. 2
Ch. 3
Ch. 4
Ch. 5
Ch. 6
Ch. 7
Ch. 8
Ch. 9
Ch. 10

1	Phrase	When it comes to ~
	Original Sentence	When it comes to the standardized college admissions tests like the SAT and ACT, there's a lot to gripe about.
	Example	When it comes to an ideal teacher, we often look into a teacher's educational background or his/her teaching experience.
	Practice	
2	Phrase	It is unclear that S + V : ~
	Original Sentence	it is unclear that standardized tests are really fair or measure actual aptitude.
	Example	It is unclear that either of them truly reflects the teacher's quality.
	Practice	
3	Phrase	Indeed,
	Original Sentence	Indeed, studies have shown that standardized test scores are less effective than things like high school grades at predicting academic performance in college, are correlated with the socioeconomic status of test takers, and are subject to the influence of coaching and private tutoring, luxuries only available to those who can afford them.

	Example	Indeed, studies have shown that a teacher's educational background does not correspond to student's academic success.
	Practice	
4	Phrase	Despite ~
	Original Sentence	Despite their many flaws, however, standardized tests are a necessary convenience for many schools, serving as a coarse method of comparison between the tens of thousands of applicants a school may consider every year.
	Example	Despite their many flaws, however, teacher's educational backgrounds are the number one consideration to most parents.
	Practice	
5	Phrase	Steps should be taken to + V:
	Original Sentence	Steps should be taken to ameliorate the importance of these tests, but getting rid of them is unfortunately not a viable option.
	Example	Steps should be taken to ameliorate an alternative such as homeschooling systems.
	Practice	
6	Phrase	The good news is that S + V :
	Original Sentence	The good news is that debate about the importance of standardized testing in college admissions finally seems to be spreading to those with the power to reform the system.
	Example	The good news is that the government starts to provide a tax break for those parents using homeschooling to their children beginning this year.
	Practice	

7	Phrase	In addition S + V :
	Original Sentence	In addition, the Commission will also propose recommendations to college admissions officers and high school counselors on how they should view standardized tests
	Example	In addition, the government is working with academics to prepare for more enhanced version of homeschooling curriculum designed under the
	Practice	
8	Phrase	Not only A ~ but also B :
	Original Sentence	not only increase admissions officers' awareness of the test's limitations, but also encourage the development of more reliable and more equitable methods of evaluation.
	Example	Not only will the parents receive the optimized version of online homeschooling curriculum, but will also interact with teachers, administration, and their kids, using their smartphone app to effectively assist their homeschooling teachers.
	Practice	
9	Phrase	To be sure
	Original Sentence	To be sure, in an ideal world, colleges would not have to rely on scores at all when evaluating applicants
	Example	To be sure, in an ideal world, traditional school system would not have to exist.
	Practice	

Ch. 1
Ch. 2
Ch. 3
Ch. 4
Ch. 5
Ch. 6
Ch. 7
Ch. 8
Ch. 9
Ch. 10

10	Phrase	Unfortunately,
	Original Sentence	unfortunately, many schools do not have the resources to implement such a costly holistic evaluation process, especially large state schools.
	Example	Unfortunately, municipal governments alone cannot implement such a costly daunting project.
	Practice	
11	Phrase	For instance,
	Original Sentence	For instance, the University of California at Los Angeles received upwards of 50,000 applications last year. Standardized tests might be a terrible system, but they are better than the alternatives.
	Example	For instance, almost all students won't listen to their parents if they did not listen to the school teachers.
	Practice	
12	Phrase	What + S + should focus on, then, is ~ not + Gerund but Gerund:
	Original Sentence	What reformers and Fitzsimmons' Commission should focus on, then, is not getting rid of standardized tests but finding ways to level the playing field within the context of the existing system.
	Example	What homeschooling should focus on, then, is not adopting all the school subjects but emphasizing on a few subjects—regardless of the subject area—that values children's preference.
	Practice	
13	Phrase	There are many ways to do so.
	Original Sentence	There are many ways to do so. The College Board, which administers the SAT, could reduce the cost of their expensive and lucrative test prep materials so that preparation becomes less of a luxury good.

	Example	There are many ways to do so. Online homeschool community could build a future career centre for the students.
	Practice	
14	Phrase	Moreover,
	Original Sentence	Moreover, colleges could share with each other information on the quality of instruction of different high schools, making it easier for deluged admissions offices to judge a student's coursework relative to standards of his or her school.
	Example	Moreover, focusing on single subject can actually reduce the school administration's budget as well as the parents'.
	Practice	
15	Phrase	In the long run,
	Original Sentence	In the long run, this would allow colleges to de-emphasize standardized testing and focus on other measures of aptitude. Such solutions would reduce the inequities
	Example	In the long run, we will get better solutions to educate children under the home-schooling system.
	Practice	

Ch. 1

Ch. 2

Ch. 3

Ch. 4

Ch. 5

Ch. 6

Ch. 7

Ch. 8

Ch. 9

Ch. 10

SAMPLE ESSAY 10

Essay Prompt

As you read the passage below, consider how THE HARVARD CRIMSON STAFF uses
 ♦ evidence, such as facts or examples, to support claims.
 ♦ reasoning to develop ideas and to connect claims and evidence.
 ♦ stylistic or persuasive elements, such as word choice or appeals to emotion, to add power to the ideas expressed.

Adopted from Adopted from <u>THE CRIMSON STAFF</u> "Cambridge is sacrificing safety by leaving its emergency surveillance cameras deactivated " Published On Friday, February 06, 2009   The Crimson, Harvard University

Privacy in our society is clearly diminishing: We carry devices everywhere we go so that people can reach us, the credit cards we use let any corporation view our purchases, and the Internet has allowed an unprecedented level of information to be publicly available.
While this trend can be troubling, simple-minded reactions are not warranted.

Unfortunately, this is exactly what happened in the Cambridge City Council on Wednesday when, following protests from many fearful and disgruntled citizens, the body voted to keep   surveillance cameras already installed in the city turned off, citing their possible contribution to the erosion of civil liberties.

This move by the council was an overreaction in light of the surveillance program's scope, purpose, and prior history. Funded by a grant from the Department of Homeland Security, a mere eight cameras were installed around Cambridge in 2008 to aid firefighters and other evacuation personnel in the event of an emergency. For a sizeable community like Cambridge, the cameras' potential to be life-saving in dire circumstances greatly outweighs their minimal impact on privacy.

Most of those in opposition to the use of these cameras at the city council meeting did not have a problem with the standard function of the cameras in emergency situations but were more concerned about the possibility of exploitation. But as much as these cameras may conjure up images of an Orwellian nightmare with the government watching our every move, they add no more cause for alarm than cameras installed on highways to monitor speed limits or in stores to monitor shoplifting. Boston has installed over 100 similar cameras already and has seen no problem in surveillance-related abuse.

While the installation process was not particularly transparent, with most of it taking place without the involvement of the Cambridge City Council, disallowing these cameras is unnecessary, rash, and wasteful. Like any newly instituted system, the cameras should be allowed a trial period with evaluation and feedback. Just as nearby Brookline agreed to activate the cameras and use them on a trial basis, Cambridge should observe the impact of cameras before making its decision.

It is a city's obligation to protect and assist its residents in a time of emergency, and blocking a possible rescue due to unfounded fears of the government being able to view a public street shows little perspective. Eight cameras will not mark the end of our First Amendment rights. Hopefully Cambridge residents will not have to wait for an accident to ensue for us to learn this.

Sample Essay 10 based on Reading / Analysis / Writing Scoring Rubric

INTRODUCTION	
1 Thesis statement	<u>In response to</u> shutting down the existing emergency surveillance cameras for privacy<u>, the writer argues that</u> the surveillance cameras should be preserved <u>in the article</u> "Cambridge is sacrificing safety by leaving its emergency surveillance cameras deactivated " <u>by appealing to persuasion, reasoning, and literary allusion.</u>
	(Title + the author's name + the central argument) ✓Demonstrates thorough comprehension of the source text ✓Shows an understanding of the text's central idea ✓Includes a skillful introduction ✓Makes skillful use of textual evidence (quotations, paraphrases or both) ✓Offers an insightful analysis of the source text ✓Offers a well-considered evaluation of the author's use of evidence, reasoning, stylistic and persuasive elements.
BODY PARAGRAPH 1	
2 Contrasting point (topic sentence)	<u>The writer starts his article off by</u> elaborating notable privacy issues in our society that are deeper and realistic than we took it for granted.
	✓Includes a precise central claim. ✓Makes skillful use of textual evidence (quotations, paraphrases or both)
3 Analysis of the thesis & Supporting details	<u>The question is, says the writer, whether</u> this trend has become so serious that we need to take a drastic action against it or still need to discuss deeper. <u>He establishes his reasoning from the opponent's view,</u> "privacy in our society is clearly diminishing"—which no one disagrees with, <u>anticipating a potential reaction against his argument.</u> He later proposes "simple-minded reactions are not warranted", <u>to progress his reasoning. This introduction paragraph provides a baseline of sorts for readers to find that there is much within the issue.</u>

3 Analysis of the thesis & Supporting details	✓Offers an insightful analysis of the source text and demonstrates a sophisticated understanding of the analytical task. ✓Offers a thorough, well-considered evaluation of the author's use of evidence, reasoning, and/or stylistic and persuasive elements, and/or feature(s) of the student's own choosing. ✓Contains relevant, sufficient, and strategically chosen support for claim(s) or point(s) made. ✓Focuses consistently on those features of the text that are most relevant to addressing the task.

BODY PARAGRAPH 2	
4 Central idea	The writer's argumentation is furthered by the recent vote by the Cambridge City Council to turn off the already installed cameras.
	✓Shows an understanding of the text's central idea(s) and of most important details and how they interrelate, demonstrating a comprehensive understanding of the text.
5 Analysis of the thesis & supporting details	He defines that the vote is made out of emotional judgment, "following protests from many fearful and disgruntled citizens,…which could jeopardize the potential life-saving opportunity in dire circumstances. He compares how much worse conditions would be without camera by presenting possible concern for the erosion of civil liberties vs. unable to aid firefighters and evacuation personals.
	✓Offers a thorough, well-considered evaluation of the author's use of evidence, reasoning, and/or stylistic and persuasive elements, and/or feature(s) of the student's own choosing. ✓Contains relevant, sufficient, and strategically chosen support for claim(s) or point(s) made. (Include - statistics- data- official names)

Ch. 1
Ch. 2
Ch. 3
Ch. 4
Ch. 5
Ch. 6
Ch. 7
Ch. 8
Ch. 9
Ch. 10

	BODY PARAGRAPH 3
6 Central Idea	Finally, the writer makes subtle yet efficient use of literary allusion," George Orwell's 1984" to persuade his audience that "Orwellian nightmare" in reality causes no more panic than cameras on highways to check speed limits or stores to catch shoplifters.
	✓Includes a precise central claim.
7 Analysis of the thesis & supporting details	His allusion inspires the reader in a way that surveillance camera can actually underperforms with possible privacy invasion, but over-performs its duty especially when in emergency situation. His strategy is definitely appealing to the reader, forcing the audience to directly compare and make judgment whether we should give up all these safety measures and security by deactivating the emergency surveillance camera in order to curve possible privacy invasion. This rational allusion surely spur some kind of response. By doing this the writer develops his argument, adding more rational persuasion to reinforce his argument and the necessity to preserve the surveillance cameras in Cambridge. In his final paragraph, the writer explicitly states that installing camera must be seen within the city's obligation to protect its residents in an emergency. Just for the sake of argument, a moral relativism of government's installing surveillance camera might be voted. However, as the writer believes, "blocking a possible rescue due to unfounded fears from privacy erosion" has little ground to debate about. The writer also cites First Amendment rights. With this seemingly exaggerated tone, instead of putting him to defend his argument on a legal ground, he utilizes as an ironic revelation to question how to properly define erosion to privacy matter. This strategy further articulates his opinion, raises more concern about deactivation of emergency cameras, while diluting the strength of opponent's perspective.
	✓The response demonstrates a consistent use of precise word choice. The response maintains a formal style and objective tone. ✓Contains relevant, sufficient, and strategically chosen support for claim(s) or point(s) made.

	CONCLUSION
8 Restate- ment of the central claim	<u>Writing as a reaction to</u> his disappointment that the city council voted to deactivate emergency surveillance camera, <u>the writer, throughout the article, elaborates his argument and discloses</u> how vulnerable the city has become by the decision. <u>Instead of building his claims by making use of full of statistics or data, the writer effectively approaches to the issue by presenting</u> literary allusion <u>based on rational judgment and insightful</u> prospects without camera.
	✓Includes a skillful introduction and conclusion. ✓The response demonstrates a deliberate and highly effective progression of ideas both within paragraphs and throughout the essay.

Ch. 1
Ch. 2
Ch. 3
Ch. 4
Ch. 5
Ch. 6
Ch. 7
Ch. 8
Ch. 9
Ch. 10

Transitional Phrase Practice

Direction

Please read the transitional phrases and the example sentences below.
Using the same phrase, create your own sentence in the practice line.
Each sentence does not have to be related to each other.

Prompt: What is the major qualification to be the best teacher?

Topic: Should a creative imitation be allowed in industry ?

1	Phrase	While …, simple-minded reactions are not warranted.
	Original Sentence.	While this trend can be troubling, simple-minded reactions are not warranted.
	Example	While creativity-oriented academics assert that copying ideas or writings of other scholars is not different from robbing someone's property, simple-minded reactions are not warranted, especially in scientific and business world.
	Practice	
2	Phrase	This move ~ was an overreaction in light of ~ 's scope, purpose, and priority. ~
	Original Sentence.	This move by the council was an overreaction in light of the surveillance program's scope, purpose, and prior history.
	Example	The move that vehemently stigmatize those who copy other scientists' idea can be an overreaction in light of possibility that more creative works can be established.
	Practice	
3	Phrase	potential ~ greatly outweighs their minimal impact on society.
	Original Sentence.	The cameras' potential to be life-saving in dire circumstances greatly outweighs their minimal impact on privacy.
	Example	Potential progress based on cooperation—which only can be materialized by utilizing everyone else's brilliant idea can greatly outweighs the minimal

	Practice	
4	Phrase	But as much as may conjure up images, they add no more cause ~
	Original Sentence.	But as much as these cameras may conjure up images of an Orwellian nightmare with the government watching our every move, they add no more cause for alarm than cameras installed on highways to monitor speed limits or in stores to monitor shoplifting.
	Example	As much as imitating others' idea may conjure up images of forgery, it adds no more cause for struggle to compete and eventually progress.
	Practice	
5	Phrase	~should observe the impact of ~ before making its decision.
	Original Sentence.	Cambridge should observe the impact of cameras before making its decision.
	Example	The government should judge the impact of comprehensive and excessively rigid copyright laws before making its decision.
	Practice	
6	Phrase	It is a ~ obligation to, and blocking a possible progress ~ due to unfounded fears of ~ shows little perspective.
	Original Sentence.	It is a city's obligation to protect and assist its residents in a time of emergency, and blocking a possible rescue due to unfounded fears of the government being able to view a public street shows little perspective.
	Example	It is government's obligation to support individual developers and creators, and blocking a possible progress due to unfounded protectionism shows little per-
	Practice	

7	Phrase	~ will not mark the end of our First Amendment rights
	Original Sentence.	Eight cameras will not mark the end of our First Amendment rights. Hopefully Cambridge residents will not have to wait for an accident to ensue for us to learn this.
	Example	Creative imitation will not mark the end of civilization enrichment progress. It will only make it better.
	Practice	

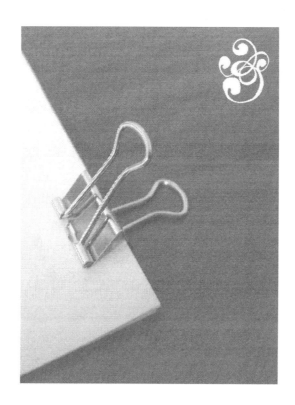

Chapter 3

Writing Introduction Paragraph

Introduction Paragraph (where you story begins and ends)

Of all the essays encompassing SAT, ACT, TOEFL, IELTS, the introduction paragraph takes on the 90% of importance on your overall essay. Therefore, your introduction paragraph must be most visible, unfold all the logic, easy to understand, and free of error. The reader must feel comfortable when start reading your introduction. Just keep in mind, your introduction should not broaden your story, which you should be located in the body paragraphs. When you use personal tone, it must be supported by logic and evidence.

The most common way to write the introduction paragraph

Start the Topic Sentence with the opposing Opinion

Step 1. Find the key word(s) from the assignment / prompt

-off topic is scored zero.

Step 2. Unfold the conclusion

- Visualize what your concluding paragraph is going to be. That is, consider what your final reaction for the question is. The question or prompt contains pros and cons. Your essay must grow out of this analysis.

Step 3. Search for antonyms and synonyms.

- By utilizing all the information such as prompt, reading passage, or out of your memory, jot down a few antonyms and synonyms that can be the backbone of your argument.

Step 4. Startup the Topic Sentence with the opposing Opinion
- Now, your topic sentence should start with the opposite opinion, acknowledging there should be another opinion or opposite argument, by doing which your introduction can provide more analytical and systemic reasoning. Do not stuff in too much on your topic sentence.

Step 5. No stage please but Detail Backup

- Without having a logical backup sentence, your topic sentence—which is supposed to be your direct opposite opinion—will lose its weigh, powerless, and sometimes nonsensical. Write one more sentence that support the topic to treat the opposite opinion looks more forcible.

Step 6. Concession &Thesis (My opinion)

- For the reader, the most favorite part is to read your thesis statement.
  You may start with a concessional phrase such as "While, Although, However, Granted that, With all due respect, In spite of, etc.
- Write your thesis only briefly.

Step 7. Summarize Your body Paragraphs

- You can optionally, but briefly, introduce your following body paragraph context.
- You can even memorize a simple sentence to save time, such as "Compelling examples can be found both in history and current event."

Introduction Example 1 starting with an opposite opinion

Original Sentence

Prompt: An Imperfect Necessity (Standardized testing may be flawed, but it is unavoidable)

When it comes to the standardized college admissions tests like the SAT and ACT, there's a lot to gripe about. Beyond bringing additional stress to the admissions process, it is unclear that standardized tests are really fair or measure actual aptitude. Indeed, studies have shown that standardized test scores are less effective than things like high school grades at predicting academic performance in college, are correlated with the socioeconomic status of test takers, and are subject to the influence of coaching and private tutoring, luxuries only available to those who can afford them. Despite their many flaws, however, standardized tests are a necessary convenience for many schools, serving as a coarse method of comparison between the tens of thousands of applicants a school may consider every year. Steps should be taken to ameliorate the importance of these tests, but getting rid of them is unfortunately not a viable option.

Structure Analysis

Topic Sentence -The Opposing Opinion	**When it comes to** the standardized college admissions tests like the SAT and ACT, there's a lot to gripe about.
Supporting Detail of the opposing Opinion	Beyond bringing additional stress to the admissions process, **it is unclear that** standardized tests are really fair or measure actual aptitude. **Indeed,** studies have shown that **standardized test scores are less effective** than things like high school grades at predicting academic performance in college, **are correlated with the socioeconomic status of test takers, and are subject to the influence of coaching and private tutoring,** luxuries only available to those who can afford them.
Concession	**Despite** their many flaws, **however,**
Thesis Statement	standardized tests **are a necessary convenience** for many schools, serving as a coarse method of comparison between the tens of thousands of applicants a school may consider every year.
Brief summary of your body paragraphs	**Steps should be taken** to ameliorate the importance of these tests, but getting rid of them is unfortunately not a viable option.

Admitting the opposing opinion should be consistent and analytical. In order to achieve this goal, you should repeatedly use the key word(s) throughout the introduction paragraph, not to mention on your body paragraphs and conclusion. By doing so, the reader will stick to your coherent opinion. To avoid redundancy or losing your tone or weigh, there should be a little bit of facelift by effectively using adjectives or adverbs around the redundant keywords. As an example, the key word in this prompt is "the standardized test", which the author uses it repeatedly throughout the passage. The author, instead of repeating it word-for-word, gives a variation like "standardized college admission tests", these testing", standardized admission testing". As seen on the above example, by giving a simple variation, you can avoid redundancy, while maintaining coherence.

Introduction Example 2 starting with an opposite opinion

Original Sentence

The Harvard Crimson
ONLINE EDITION

Prompt: Press the On Button

Cambridge is sacrificing safety by leaving its emergency surveillance cameras deactivated

Privacy in our society is clearly diminishing: We carry devices everywhere we go so that people can reach us, the credit cards we use let any corporation view our purchases, and the Internet has allowed an unprecedented level of information to be publicly available. While this trend can be troubling, simple-minded reactions are not warranted.

Structure Analysis

Topic Sentence The Opposing Opinion	Privacy in our society is clearly diminishing:
Supporting Detail of the opposing Opinion	We carry devices everywhere we go so that people can reach us, the credit cards we use let any corporation view our purchases, and the Internet has allowed an unprecedented level of information to be publicly available.
Concession	**While** this trend can be troubling,
Thesis Statement	**simple-minded reactions are not warranted.**

 Ch. 1
 Ch. 2
 Ch. 3
 Ch. 4
 Ch. 5
 Ch. 6
 Ch. 7
 Ch. 8
 Ch. 9
 Ch. 10

Introduction Example 3 Starting with An Opposite Opinion

Original Sentence

Assignment: Do we need to give more attention to elders because they are more experienced than we are?

Learning from the elders' experience *is critical to establish and maintain successful society.* Their empirical experience would reduce any possible mistakes—big and small--we can make, while acting as a reliable navigational tool to chart our future. *With all due respect, history has witnessed* that civilization progressed through revolutionary minds, especially through those who followed iconoclastic and clairvoyant perspectives, casting away rules set and preconditioned by elders. Thus, **it is pivotal** that we maintain ourselves be progressive while paying attention to elders' experience.

Structure Analysis

Topic Sentence The Opposing Opinion	Learning from the elders' experience *is critical to establish and maintain successful society.*
Supporting Detail of the opposing Opinion	Their empirical experience would reduce any possible mistakes—big and small--we can make, while acting as a reliable navigational tool to chart our future.
Concession	*With all due respect, history has witnessed* that civilization progressed through revolutionary minds, especially through those who followed iconoclastic and clairvoyant perspectives, casting away rules set and preconditioned by elders.
Thesis Statement	Thus, **it is pivotal** that we maintain ourselves be progressive while paying attention to elders' experience.

Introduction Paragraph Practice 1

Write your own Introduction Paragraph using the same topic, but with the opposite opinion.

Assignment :Do we need to give more attention to elders because they are more experienced than we are?

You may use the following phrases

1. ~ *is critical to establish and maintain successful society.*

2. *With all due respect, however,*

3.*It is pivotal that we*

Topic	
Detail	
Concession	
Thesis (my opinion)	
A brief Summary for the body paragraphs	

Tip: By simply switching important to other synonyms, your thesis can look a lot sophisticated. Use such as Pivotal, imperative, critical, significant, essential, integral, vital, primal

Introduction Example 4 Starting with An Opposite Opinion

Original Sentence

Assignment: Do we need to give more attention to elders because they are more experienced than we are?

When thinking of older generations, **we quite often consider** they are lethargic, and a disposed or near-disposed group in society. The functional ethos inveterate in our society is that they should consume less because they earn less and contribute lesser as some complain that social welfare backed by taxpayer's money withdraws money to be spent on education for children for their future. **Although** their contribution to society may seem trivial from the economic point of view, the intangible hands-on experience they possess and can teach us would play no less important role than money, and surely would function as even more integral element in society.

Compelling examples both from literature and history explicitly support this thesis.

Structure Analysis

Topic Sentence The Opposing Opinion	**When thinking of** older generations, **we quite often consider** they are lethargic, and a disposed or near-disposed group in society.
Supporting Detail of the opposing Opinion	The functional ethos inveterate in our society is that they should consume less because they earn less and contribute lesser as some complain that social welfare backed by taxpayer's money withdraws money to be spent on education for children for their future.
Concession	**Although** their contribution to society may seem trivial from the economic point of view,
Thesis Statement	the intangible hands-on experience they possess and can teach us would play no less important role than money, and surely would function as even more integral element in society.
Brief Summary of your Body Paragraphs	**Compelling examples both from literature and history explicitly support this thesis.**

Introduction Paragraph Practice 2

Write your own Introduction Paragraph using the same topic, but with the opposite opinion.

Assignment :Do we need to give more attention to elders because they are more experienced than we are?	
You may use the following phrases *1. When thinking of ... we often consider ...* *2. Although, ... plays no less important role in ....* *3. Compelling examples both from literature and history explicitly support this thesis.*	
Topic	
Detail	
Concession	
Thesis (my opinion)	
A brief Summary for the body paragraphs	

Introduction Example 4 Starting with An Opposite Opinion

Original Sentence

Assignment: Modern technology is creating a single world culture.

Without a doubt, modern technology has provided enhanced and comprehensive vision for advancement that allows all humanitarian to explore and gather information with the infinite size that seemed unthinkable decades ago. **Underpinning** the internet, global economy, politics, and even culture have become a single entity that combines all nations to rely on each other. **Granted that** yearning for a single global community is admirable dream, **it is also evident that** we are losing cultural diversity, creating inequality and hierarchical orders among countries and cultures. Alongside dreams of transhumanism, **doubt lingers whether** we can combine the entire races, religions, and cultures.

Structure Analysis

Topic Sentence The Opposing Opinion	**Without a doubt,** modern technology has provided enhanced and comprehensive vision for advancement that allows all humanitarian to explore and gather information with the infinite size that seemed unthinkable decades ago.
Supporting Detail of the opposing Opinion	**Underpinning** the internet, global economy, politics, and even culture have become a single entity that combines all nations to rely on each other.
Concession	**Granted that** yearning for a single global community is admirable dream,
Thesis Statement	**it is also evident that** we are losing cultural diversity, creating inequality and hierarchical orders among countries and cultures. Alongside dreams of transhumanism, **doubt lingers whether** we can combine the entire races, religions, and cultures.

Introduction Paragraph Practice 3

Write your own Introduction Paragraph using the same topic, but with the opposite opinion.

Assignment :Modern technology is creating a single world culture.

You may use the following phrases

1. **Without a doubt,**

2. **Underpinning** ...

3. **Granted that ...**

4. **it is also evident that ...**

5. **doubt lingers whether...**

Topic	
Detail	
Concession	
Thesis (my opinion)	

Starting the Topic Sentence with Your Thesis

Instead of starting the topic sentence with antithesis, you may initiate your own thesis. Please follow the procedures below.

Step 1. Find the key word(s) from the assignment / prompt

-off topic is scored zero.

Step 2. Unfold the conclusion

- Visualize what your concluding paragraph is going to be. That is, consider what your final reaction for the question is. The question or prompt contains pros and cons. Your essay must grow out of this analysis.

Step 3. Search for antonyms and synonyms.

- By utilizing all the information such as prompt, reading passage, or out of your memory, jot down a few antonyms and synonyms that can be the backbone of your argument.

Step 4. **Startup the Topic Sentence with the main concern (the prompt)**
- Your topic sentence should present what the main concern is. Do not stuff in too much on your topic sentence.

Ch. 1

Ch. 2

Ch. 3

Ch. 4

Ch. 5

Ch. 6

Ch. 7

Ch. 8

Ch. 9

Ch. 10

Step 5. No stage please but Detail Backup

- Without having a logical backup sentence, your topic sentence will lose its weigh, powerless, and sometimes nonsensical.   Write one more sentence that support the topic to treat the following thesis looks more forcible.

Step 6. Summarize Your body Paragraphs

- You can optionally, but briefly, introduce your following body paragraph contexts.

- You can even memorize a simple sentence to save time, such as "Compelling examples can be found both in history and current event."

1. Intelligent Machines (source: ACT.org)

Many of the goods and services we depend on daily are now supplied by intelligent, automated machines rather than human beings. Robots build cars and other goods on assembly lines, where once there were human workers. Many of our phone conversations are now conducted not with people but with sophisticated technologies. We can now buy goods at a variety of stores without the help of a human cashier. Automation is generally seen as a sign of progress, but what is lost when we replace humans with machines? Given the accelerating variety and prevalence of intelligent machines, it is worth examining the implications and meaning of their presence in our lives.

Perspective One: What we lose with the replacement of people by machines is some part of our own humanity. Even our mundane daily encounters no longer require from us basic courtesy, respect, and tolerance for other people.

Perspective Two: Machines are good at low-skill, repetitive jobs, and at high-speed, extremely precise jobs. In both cases they work better than humans. This efficiency leads to a more prosperous and progressive world for everyone.

Perspective Three: Intelligent machines challenge our long-standing ideas about what humans are or can be. This is good because it pushes both humans and machines toward new, unimagined possibilities.

Write a unified, coherent essay in which you evaluate multiple perspectives on the increasing presence of intelligent machines.

Introduction Example 4 Starting with Your Thesis

Original Sentence

Assignment: Write a unified, coherent essay in which you evaluate multiple perspectives on the increasing presence of intelligent machines.

The idea that we can depend on the intelligent machines in the entire system is emerging. **In fact,** many enthusiastic public, industries, even the conservative intelligentsia —journalists, think-tankers, and academics—have surrendered to machine dominancy. **It may seem conspicuous that** to resist in this trends is not a good option. **With all due respect,** the manifesto that intelligent machines will restore the defects of their own and promise unifying harmony with human workers will most likely generate a fatal consequence.

Structure Analysis

Topic Sentence The main concern	**The idea that** we can depend on the intelligent machines in the entire system is emerging.
Supporting Detail	**In fact**, many enthusiastic public, industries, even the conservative intelligentsia —journalists, think-tankers, and academics—have surrendered to machine dominancy. **It seems conspicuous that** to resist in this trends is not a good option.
Concession	**With all due respect,**
Thesis Statement	the manifesto that intelligent machines will restore the defects of their own and promise unifying harmony with human workers will most likely generate a fatal consequence.

Introduction Paragraph Practice 3

Write your own Introduction Paragraph using the same topic, but with the opposite opinion.

Assignment: Write a unified, coherent essay in which you evaluate multiple perspectives on the increasing presence of intelligent machines.

You may use the following phrases

1. **The idea that ….**

2. **In fact,** …

3. **It may seem conspicuous that**

4. **With all due respect,**

5. **Thesis**

Topic	
Detail	
Concession	
Thesis (my opinion)	

HARVARD STUDENT ESSAY ANALAYS

Ch. 1

Ch. 2

Ch. 3

Ch. 4

Ch. 5

Ch. 6

Ch. 7

Ch. 8

Ch. 9

Ch. 10

San's SAT ESSAY HACKERS

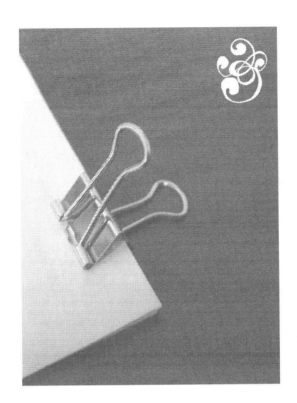

Chapter 4

Writing Body Paragraph

Body Paragraph

The Function of Body Paragraph

The body paragraphs work in coalition with your introduction paragraph, based upon which you further elaborate the thesis with evidential and logical examples.

The number of Body Paragraph

Unless college paper requires a certain length of your essay, most of the college entrance exams requires no more than two ~ three body paragraphs.

The Layout of Your Body Paragraph

Your body paragraph must contain topic, subtopic (s), evidential example (s).
You should practice what to write on your first sentence, second, and the third, and after. Developing the formulated body paragraph can let you reduce possible mistakes such as syntax error, spelling error, coherence error, redundant error, and so on. It is highly recommended not to exceed more than 10 sentences on each body paragraph.

Body Paragraph 1

On your body paragraph 1, you should deliver the main concern or the background information only that supports the assignment given. Within it you, should proceed the information with what is currently being examined, occurring, and widely accepted.

Body Paragraph 2

The development of issue or problem is the main difference that borders the body paragraph 2 from the body paragraph 1. You should not repeat the background information that is already stated on your body paragraph 1. You should only offer the problem (s). How the background information generates problem or response. You should facilitate problems with evidence. Just keep in mind, if you restate the background information, you are going to kill both the body paragraph 1 and 2.

Ch. 1

Ch. 2

Ch. 3

Ch. 4

Ch. 5

Ch. 6

Ch. 7

Ch. 8

Ch. 9

Ch. 10

Body Paragraph 3

The sole purpose of your body paragraph 3 is to settle the conflicts, problems, issues that have been stated throughout body paragraph 1 and 2. You should not resume the issue or problem stated on body paragraph 2, which should have been ended on your previous paragraph. You can state solution, negotiate with the reader, persuade support from the reader. Just keep in mind, do not drag even deeper problems here, which will require additional paragraph to deal with this new issue.

Fatal Mistakes That You Can Do To Your Body Paragraph

1. Write more than one subject

- Writing more than one subject at limited time and space can kill each other. You can write hundreds of subject in one body paragraph that loosens connection. Aiming and refueling a single subject in one body paragraph will make your statement deeper and more influential.

2. Write cliché

- Start your body paragraph with "In my opinion", "I strongly believe that", or starting each paragraph with "First", "Second", In today's society" or "Many people think that.... The reader already knows that it is your opinion and you strongly believe that…" such a cliché will make your statement less your opinion because the reader knows the cliché comes from your memorization.

3. Write Your Opinion Without Evidence, Fact, Data

- Without having a specific evidence, elaborating your opinion makes it powerless, incoherent, illogical, unanalytical. Consider this example.

  A) Russia bears the heaviest responsibility for inflaming the conflict in Northern Europe.

  B) Russia, beginning the air war in 2015 with the aim of reinstalling satellite countries, bears the heaviest responsibility for inflaming the conflict in Northern Europe.

4. Change your mind

More often than not, many students drastically change their opinion within the paragraph—very deliberately. This mistake arises—I suspect, not from lack of reasoning, but from misdirected belief that the reader will appreciate the intelligent of the writer. Targeting one subject to become both your friend and enemy is intelligent.

5. Inject an issue not related with the prompt (Question).

Even though the example that comes up to your mind is very tempting to fill the gap, while minimizing time, effort, and possible mistakes, your essay will be ousted mercilessly from the reader if it is definitely off-topic.

6. Write Vague, unfocused statements

The prompt (question)—more often than not, does not give you the precise conclusion, rather it is vague, ambiguous that requires your specific analysis. Without specifying the question, if you simply follow the prompt given, your essay will also be vague and unfocused. Trust me, even you wouldn't understand what you wrote yourself. To make your statement and analysis clear, memorize a few exemplary cases to be utilized in many different issues(Question).

As an example, please refer to the following question conversion.

> The Original Prompt: Is it better for a society when people act as individuals rather than copying the ideas and opinions of others?
>
> The Question Conversion: copyright infringement is illegal conduct; however, unlike artistic world, scientific and technological idea must be shared in order to progress.

> The Original Prompt: Do we have to accept the fact that the biological difference between women and men should be applied in society?
>
> The Question Conversion: The legal acceptance that women and men are equal is less than a hundred year old concept. Susan Antony and the escaped slave, Fredrick Douglas were the main activists in the movements in early 1900s.

The Original Prompt: Do people need to "unlearn," or reject, many of their assumptions and ideas?

The Question Conversion: some opponents raise issue on environmental catastrophe. They reason that environment protection Acts have made much progress and wide spread concerns are somewhat overblown by the extreme environmentalists and populistic politicians.

Writing Body Paragraph with evidence

Step 1. Think likely nominees to be used in your body paragraph

Consider what example fits the best in the assignment. Before the exam, you should be prepared to study several examples that encompass, to name of a few, humanity, science, technology, leadership, history, art.

Example

*To Kill A Mockingbird

*Load of the Flies

*Hamlet

*Macbeth

*World War II

*Bill Gates

*Galileo Galilei

*Steve Jobs

*ISIS and terrorism

Step 2. The specific items that should be included in your example

A full of example without evidence does not appeal to the reader. A strong opinion must be supported by strong evidence like a potato chip with full of nitrogen, but little chips. As an example, if you decided to write your example using Macbeth, you should remember the following:

1. Title: Macbeth

2. Author: William Shakespeare

3. Protagonist: Macbeth

4. Antagonists & other Characters: Lady Macbeth, King Duncan, Macduff, three witches Banquo, Prince, Malcolm, Duncan's son

5 Approximate years

6. Theme: Man's desire unchecked by morale can disintegrate his status quo.

7. Main Event:

    1) . Upon arrival to Scotland after the consecutive victory at the battle, Macbeth and Banquo encounters trio of witches, learning that Macbeth will be the King of Scotland.

    2). With Lady Macbeth's encouragement, Macbeth stabs King Duncan to realize witches' prophecy.

    3) Macduff, Prince Malcolm, the Son of King Duncan fled to England and later learn that Macduff's heirs and wife get murdered by Macbeth.

    4) Scottish nobles support Macduff because of Macbeth's tyrannical and murderous behavior.

    5) Lady Macbeth, gone mad, kills herself.

    6) . Macduff kills and beheads Macbeth.

<u>8</u>. Analysis (Introspection & Retrospection)

    If the earlier sentence involves the evidence, Now you should inspire your reader with reasoning. That is, you should associate your reader by reviewing the fact, denying the fact, accepting the fact. As an example, you could use the conditional "if clause" on your analysis, announcing what something or someone could have been done.

9. Analysis Backup (Prediction)

    On your analysis, write what you could predict in the future.

    Ex) When ambition falls upon the shoulders of a man without judicious evaluation between right and wrong, his incapability will beget irreversible results.

Body Paragraph 1 Example A

Think carefully about the issue presented in the following excerpt and the assignment below.
When someone has the same ideas or views as most people do, we tend to believe that the person is reasonable and correct. Often, however, views that are considered reasonable or commonsensical are anything but sensible. Many widely held views regarding current events, science, education, arts and literature, and many other topics ultimately prove to be wrong. The fact that an idea or view is widespread—held by many people—does not make it right.

Assignment: Is conscience a more powerful motivator than money, fame or power?

Using "Macbeth"

Topic	**One example that clarifies that** (man's desire unchecked by morale disintegrates his status quo: *Theme)* **can be found in** (a tragic protagonist Macbeth : *the Protagonist)* **in the play Macbeth by** (William Shakespeare : *Author)*
Author's perspective	**Shakespeare uses (Macbeth :** the protagonist**) to show** (how destructively powerful as well as volatile human conscious can be when confronted with delectable challenge.
Story Line	**In this play,** upon arrival to Scotland after the consecutive victory at the vicious battle, Macbeth and Banquo encounters trio of witches, learning that Macbeth will be the King of Scotland. With Lady Macbeth's encouragement, Macbeth stabs King Duncan to realize witches' prophecy. Macduff, Prince Malcolm, the Son of King Duncan fled to England and later learn that Macduff's heirs and wife get murdered by Macbeth. Scottish nobles support Macduff because of Macbeth's tyrannical and murderous behavior. Lady Macbeth, gone mad, kills herself. Macduff kills and beheads Macbeth.
Analysis	**Had** Macbeth **not followed** three witches' prophecy and remained firm in his belief as an intellectual man, **he would not have** created turmoil and tragedy not only to himself, but also to the entire county.
Analysis backup	**As seen on the above analysis,** When ambition falls upon the shoulders of a man unattained by lack of judicious evaluation, his incapability will beget irreversible results.

Body paragraph 1 Practice

Choose your own example and practice below.

Topic Sentence	One example that clarifies... can be found in …
Author's perspective	The author uses … to show
Story Line 3~6 Sentences	In this novel...
Analysis	
Analysis Backup	As seen on the above analysis,,,,

Body Paragraph 1 Example B

Assignment: Is conscience a more powerful motivator than money, fame or power?

Using "Load of the Flies"

Topic	**The theme that** conscious—whether good or bad—becomes most powerful motivator) **is also illustrated throughout William Golding's signature novel Load of the Flies.**
Author's perspective	**Golding reveals that** the savagery instinct is deepest principle that controls human psyche than moral. **The idea of** human's inherent desire for power and evil conduct **is central to** load of the flies.
Story Line	When WWII was nearing to the end, a plane boarded a group of boys who were evacuating from London is shot down in a deserted island. The main protagonist, Ralph as an appointed leader attempts to support the rest of the boys to be safely rescued by building a civilized island. The main antagonist, Jack who becomes the hunters' tribe leader desires for power, representing the innate savagery within human. The rest of the boys who initially followed Ralph become increasingly wild and barbaric. As the title, Load of the Flies symbolizes, sow's head dominates boys' psyche and human civilization, Eventually, Roger by rolling a boulder down the mountain, killing Piggy and shattering the conch shell—disintegrates human's morale and civilization.
Analysis	**Of course, this is not to say that** human's instinct is brutal and barbaric, so it can't be moderated. Main protagonist Ralph and Simon, and piggy maintain moral disciplined behavior while Jack and his hunters' tribe get used to brutal, barbaric life.
Analysis backup	**The example illustrated by the main protagonist, Ralph and antagonist Jack provides evidence that** the main concern of the Load of the Flies is the competing impulses that exist in human: civilization vs. savagery, law vs. anarchy, and good vs. evil

Body Paragraph 2 Example A

Topic	**The theme** whether conscious is more powerful motivator than money or fame **is not limited to literary examples. We can see this immutable principle throughout history as well. Consider** Galileo Galilei **if you will**
Story Line	Dazzling technological advancement we are witnessing today would never have been possible without scientific revolution Galileo Galilei had unwrapped. Though remained as the father of modern science by contributing physics, astronomy, and broad range of physiology, support for Copernicanism was his lifetime controversial shackle. When a large majority of philosophers and astronomers still advocated to the geocentric view that the Earth is at the center of the universe, after 1610, when he began publicly supporting the heliocentric view, which placed the Sun at the center of the universe, he met with bitter opposition from the Catholic dominated world in which his Helio-centricism was condemned as false and found vehemently suspect of heresy. Eventually, because of his most famous work, "Dialogue Concerning the two chief world systems", Galileo spent the rest of his life under the house arrest.
Analysis	**The above described historical event of** Galileo Galilei explicitly **suggest that** as long as integrity for his or her desire remains intact, fruitful result will always be guaranteed.
Analysis backup	His tacit word "the earth does move" figuratively and literarily set the millstone of modern physics, astronomy, and physiology. He opened the night sky and allowed us to human understanding. **Without** his contribution and sacrifice, human civilization **would have been** delayed for centuries, if not forever.

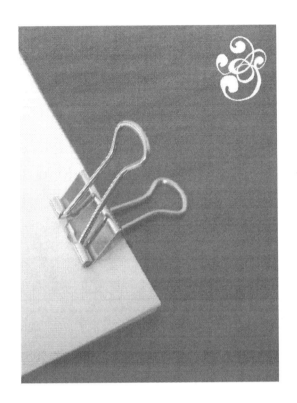

Chapter 5

Writing Conclusion Paragraph

Conclusion Paragraph

The Function of Conclusion Paragraph

The conclusion paragraphs work in coalition with your introduction paragraph and body paragraphs based upon which you summarize the thesis.

The Layout of Your Body Paragraph

Your conclusion paragraph must contain topic and thesis.

Basically it is to rephrase of your introduction paragraph.

Developing the formulated conclusion paragraph can let you reduce possible mistakes such as syntax error, spelling error, coherence error, redundant error, and so on. It is highly recommended not to exceed more than five sentences.

Topic Sentence Examples

1. As revealed in his speech in the shadow of the Lincoln Memorial, King highlights …..

2. As described by Machiavelli, rigid tendency cling to honesty can hinder constant success. Therefore, one must change his conduct according to situation.

3. In his work Concepts of Corporation , Drucker explicitly describes that ...

Sample Essay Starting with Your Thesis

Assignment: Write a unified, coherent essay in which you evaluate multiple perspectives on the increasing presence of intelligent machines.

The idea that we can depend on the intelligent machines in the entire system in our society is emerging. **In fact**, many enthusiastic public, industries, even the conservative intelligentsia — journalists, think-tankers, and academics—have surrendered to machine dominancy. **It may seem conspicuous that** to resist in this trends is not a good option. **With all due respect,** the manifesto that intelligent machines will restore the defects of their own and promise unifying harmony with human workers will most likely generate a fatal consequence.

As modern society is rapidly approaching to technocracy, there is hardly any industry that hesitates to adopt fully automated, intelligent machines in their workplaces.
Think, for a moment, about your daily living. You might find the miniature version of intelligent machine dominated society, to name a few: automated recoding voice, email transactions, instant money transfer to your grandma, best restaurant review for your dinner through smartphone. When such a progress is the norm of our society, it feeds on itself. We trust machines and trivialize any sacrifice will pay off by itself because what we get from the mechanized society looks so much larger.

Now, imagine a different reality: one in which your family—or whole community where you live—must be involved. Because your boss trust intelligent machines as much as, if not more than, you do, you should accept his decision to replace your, your wife's, your father's, and mother's job with less frustration. Because the machine simply rewards more to your boss while expecting less salary. According to a recent survey at Washington Post, middle-class wealth has shrunk by 90 percent compared to two decades ago. Many American middle class families are no longer confident in their children's future living standards says the report. While school provides a better education system to our children—of course with the help of intelligent machines such as online education, smartphone education apps, enhanced interactions between teachers and parents through emails that have drastically reduced modern illiteracy rate, our positive perspective on our children have been faded with current unstable job markets, rapidly replaced by intelligent machines. It seems to be true that more advanced life style can be materialized by implementing intelligent machines. However, a variety of polls suggest we should expect our children to be worsen off.

Now, it is time to re-consider a substantial trade-off we confront due to intelligent machines as it becomes obvious that losing jobs cannot make our lives better off.

While employers enjoy a higher return by implementing intelligent machines and by laying off human workers, they should realize a large segments of workers are the customers of other industries as well.

Legislators and academics along with the industries must cope with the single plan to benefit middle and low-income families and protect them from intelligent machine dominated economy. Allowing them to access the same quality information, education, and entertainment is essential. After all, the advent of intelligent machine-dominated society is to let us enjoy rising living standards.

The realm of humanity like artists, writers, entertainers is cultural that cannot be possessed by understanding of intelligent machines. Underpinning this natural theme lives human.

Ch. 1
Ch. 2
Ch. 3
Ch. 4
Ch. 5
Ch. 6
Ch. 7
Ch. 8
Ch. 9
Ch. 10

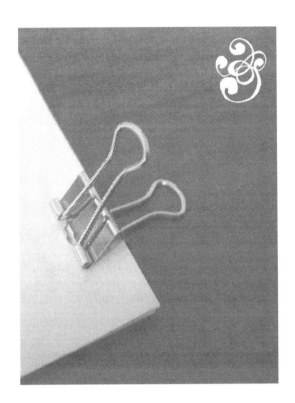

Chapter 6

Essay Formats

ESSAY FORMAT

Creating Essay can be very challenging, especially when we encounter a tough assignment. In fact, most SAT/ACT/TOEFL/IELTS essays do not expect from students to create an exquisite, timeless work of art. Instead, it is, more often than not, opposite: mechanical, subject-focused analysis. Therefore, you should demonstrate your ability to write an essay that does not fit into a broad definition of literature, but rather an essay within a densely analyzed work that precisely interprets the assignment.
Following samples show how you can formulate your essay within the scope of assignment requirements.

Directions: Please read the following three articles. Then, review how three different articles are formulated, re-manufactured within the format.

SAT ESSAY FORUMAR SUMMARY

INTRODUCTION

INCLUDE:	In response to (TITLE) , writer (THE NAME OF THE AUTHOR) argues that (THESIS) (THE AUTHOR'S ARTICLE) " (ASSIGNMENT) " is effectively built upon through the contemplation of (MAIN THEME WITH STYLISTIC & ANALTYICAL DEVICES) . (THE AUTHOR)' overall purpose in writing this article appears to be to draw attention towards (THE AUTHOR'S MAIN ARGUMENT RESTATEMENT), in which sense (THE AUTHOR'S) article is persuasive ~ to the audience.

* Title
* Author's Name
* Thesis
* Assignment
* Main Theme With
   Stylistic Devices
* Main Argument
   Restatement
 	
(Persuasion)	

BODY PARAGRAPH 1

INCLUDE:	In his introduction, (THE AUTHOR) starts with (INTRO.SUMMARY). (THE AUTHOR) utilizes (INTRODUCTION SUMMARY RESTATMENT) to later support his argument by convincingly revealing the fact that (FACT, DATA, EVIDENCE IN THE CONCLUSION PARAGRAPH). Such a phrase forces the reader to question that (THESIS). By delivering (INTRO.SUMMARY), the author leads the reader with more credence to his view.

* Introduction
   Summary
*Introduction
   Restatement Or
   Paraphrase
*Fact, Data,
   Evidence Found In
   The Conclusion
   Paragraph
*Persuasion	

SAT ESSAY FORUMAR SUMMARY

Ch. 1
Ch. 2
Ch. 3
Ch. 4
Ch. 5
Ch. 6
Ch. 7
Ch. 8
Ch. 9
Ch. 10

BODY PARAGRAPH 2

INCLUDE:

* Transitional Phrase To Link The Paragraph 1
* Fact, Data, Evidence
* Another Fact, Data, Evidence
* Concluding Analysis Of The Fact, Data, Evidence.
* Stylistic Devices Or Word Choices
* Argument With The Author's Intention

Followed by his analysis on (TRANSIONAL PHRASE TO LINK THE PARAGRAPH 1), (THE AUTHOR) further solidifies his argument, bringing (FACT, DATA, EVIDENCE) into his analytic argument. As an example, (EXAMPLE OR QUOATION) (THE AUTHOR) employs (ANOTHER FACT, DATA, EVIDENCE).

(THE AUTHOR)'S analysis gains competent evidence to back up his argument. Using (ANOTHER FACT, DATA, EVIDENCE) ensure the reader to accept the facts that he presents without prejudice. At the end of academic analysis, he concludes that (ANALYSIS)

His reliance on the usage of (STYLISTIC DEVICES or WORD CHOICES) is insightful in that (ARGUMENT WITH THE AUTHOR'S INTENTION)

SAT ESSAY FORUMAR SUMMARY

BODY PARAGRAPH 3

| INCLUDE:

-Transitional Phrase Linking The Paragraph 2

-Intro. Of Body 3

-Fact, Data, Evidence, Quotation

-Analysis

-Stylistic Devices, Word Choices

-Persuasion | Finally, (THE AUTHOR) encourages the reader to view this less impressive correlation from a broader perspective. (THRANSITIONAL PHRASE LINKING THE PARAGRAPH 2)
(THE AUTHOR) introduces (INTRO. OF BODY 3).
(THE AUTHOR) also warns that ~ (FACT, DATA, EVIDENCE, QUOTATION). He further suggests that (ANALYSIS). His series of elaboration reflects (ANALYSIS). In this regards, (THE AUTHOR'S) his judicious analytic inclusion of (STYLISTIC DEVICES, WORD CHOICES) requires us to evaluate this article without simple minded reaction. (PERSUASION) |

SAT ESSAY FORUMAR SUMMARY

CONCLUSION

INCLUDE:	
-Appeal To The Reader -Thesis Restatement -Analysis –Stylistic Devices, Word Choices -Persuasion	**To sum up**, (THE AUTHOR)'s article that encompasses his analytical skills, and deductive reasoning greatly appeal to the reader. (APPEAL TO THE READER) (THE AUTHOR) renders the audience to observe the ~ (THESIS). In an effort to persuade his audience, (THE AUTHOR) ~ . Rather, he sends a unqualified remarks with ~ to bolster his analysis. (ALAYSIS) His approach is quintessential because it insightfully protects his argument mainly by ~ (STYLISTIC DEVICES, WORD CHOICES) articulating how critics believe about the issue, in which he cogently leads the reader to view the issue with deeper insight. Therefore, it is clear that his argument is exceptionally persuasive in dealing with such a debatable issue. (PERSUASION)

SAMPLE ESSAY 1

Essay Prompt

As you read the passage below, consider how Idrees M. Kahloon uses

♦ evidence, such as facts or examples, to support claims.

♦ reasoning to develop ideas and to connect claims and evidence.

♦ stylistic or persuasive elements, such as word choice or appeals to emotion, to add power to the ideas expressed.

Adopted from Idrees M. Kahloon "Are democracy and constitutional Islam at odds?"
© January 29, 2016 The Crimson, Harvard University

Before the man was deposed, Egyptian President Mohamed Morsi was roundly derided for ramrodding through a new constitution that would have, as his critics charged, made Egypt into an illiberal theocracy. Of special consternation was its second article, which declared that "Islam is the religion of the state and Arabic its official language. Principles of Islamic Sharia are the principal source of legislation." But when Egypt's next constitution, shepherded in by the military and ratified as Morsi stood trial, was found to contain nearly-identical language, the bells of discontent were not rung quite so loud.

Meanwhile, Western nations were recently involved in rewriting the Iraqi and Afghani constitutions, both of which prominently enshrined the position of Islam. Does this analysis affirm the warning that "the elevation of Iranian-style theocrats," as one critical academic put it at the time, would undo the democratic order?

Here, the familiar chiding about correlation and causation need be remembered. Between the high-minded sphere of constitutional design and actual, day-to-day impact on residents lies the apparatus of censors, judges, and policemen who modulate constitutional demands and translate them for the common man. What constitutions prescribe and what bureaucracies end up dealing out can be quite different. Though constitutionally secular, Indonesia has strong anti-blasphemy laws and government-sanctioned persecution against religious minorities.

Academics have also proposed explanations for these Islamic provisions that could complicate matters. So-called "repugnancy clauses," which invalidate laws judged contradictory to Islam and are perhaps the strongest endorsements of religion, are thought to have originated with British rule of India, when the imperial government gave itself the power to overrule legislation "repugnant to the laws of England." And it is often the relatively liberal regimes that introduce Islamist provisions, like Egyptian President Anwar Sadat did in the country's 1971 constitution, probably in an attempt to consolidate power and legitimize themselves before conservatives.

Nonetheless, as the rash of revolution in the Middle East is sure to be followed by a rash of constitution drafting, it's important to know the crowd-pleasers, like acknowledging Islam to be the religion of the state, from the more serious clauses that require all legislation or judicial decisions to have religious approval.

Imagine if Goldilocks were to go constitution-picking. She would settle on something not too theocratic, not too secular. In the Muslim world, that may be just right.

SAMPLE ESSAY 2

Essay Prompt

As you read the passage below, consider how Lily K. Calcagnini uses

♦ evidence, such as facts or examples, to support claims.

♦ reasoning to develop ideas and to connect claims and evidence.

♦ stylistic or persuasive elements, such as word choice or appeals to emotion, to add power to the ideas expressed.

Adopted from Lily K. Calcagnini *"Fashion marketing moves from billboards to museum displays*
" © November 20, 2015 The Crimson, Harvard University

Last October, LVMH allocated $143 million to found a private museum of contemporary art for its Louis Vuitton Foundation, and commissioned architect Frank Gehry to design and construct it in Paris's Bois de Boulogne. Even for the multinational conglomerate that runs Louis Vuitton, Moët, Hennessy, and 66 other luxury goods companies—all of which you've definitely heard of—this is a considerable investment worth investigating.

What merits a price tag of $143 million? In part, social capital. When prompted to explain why he wished to open the Louis Vuitton Foundation, Bernard Arnault, the CEO of LVMH,said, "We wanted to present Paris with an extraordinary space for art and culture, and demonstrate daring and emotion by entrusting Frank Gehry with the construction of an iconic building for the 21st century."

Indeed, Arnault was able to successfully build his museum on a plot of land that had previously been denied to several other land developers. While these competitors wished to construct office buildings and business centers, Arnault was granted control of the land because his proposition was deemed to be a noble endeavor to create a public work.
But in a city that already boasts high concentrations of both art and culture, this was an ambitious— maybe even superfluous—undertaking.

It's clear to me that the goal of creating a rich, new ground for cultural discovery was only of secondary importance to Arnault. Though the museum has staged several provoking shows recently, in its opening weeks it showed nothing more than a condensed version of Arnault's private collection.

Though endeavors like these legitimize fashion as a mode of artistic production, they also render haute couture inaccessible to the masses. Museums showcase things that are untouchable, difficult to parse, and furthermore things that cannot be owned. Though naming a museum of contemporary art after Louis Vuitton ties the brand to culture, the effect is more complex.

Additionally, museums physically separate consumers from clothing. Though I'm already alienated by the four-figured price tag on a Chanel dress, I feel even more unworthy of owning it when that dress must be protected from my touch by glass cases and security ropes.

Though I seriously believe that fashion belongs in museums, it seems that this is not the most effective marketing tactic. However, there does seem to be a way to create museums solely dedicated to clothes that is not alienating, but rather inviting.

Valentino Garavani, owner and designer of the eponymous high-end label, has done so by founding a museum that won't cost him any overhead. In 2011, Garavani and his partner Giancarlo Giammetti launched the Valentino Garavani Virtual Museum, a website and accompanying downloadable applet that provides viewers with unlimited, free access to 50 years of the label's haute couture archives. Featuring cutting-edge, immersive 3-D, the virtual museum allows anyone to interactively explore over 5,000 dresses—their cut, materials, history, and production information.

In comparison to the Louis Vuitton Foundation, Valentino's virtual gallery seems much more honest. LVMH's new museum may indeed be a beautiful gift to the art world and a lovely amenity for Parisians, but as a surreptitious marketing attempt, it is ultimately nothing more than sponsored content. And while The Fondazione Prada purports only to add to its foundress's empire, I'm interested to see how its opening affects the revenue of the clothing brand that bears her name.

SAMPLE ESSAY 3

Essay Prompt

As you read the passage below, consider how **Shubhankar Chhokra** uses

♦ evidence, such as facts or examples, to support claims.

♦ reasoning to develop ideas and to connect claims and evidence.

♦ stylistic or persuasive elements, such as word choice or appeals to emotion, to add power to the ideas expressed.

Adopted from Shubhankar Chhokra "Obama's Disillusioned Doctrine" © March 25, 2016
The Crimson, Harvard University

Next month's cover story for The Atlantic is the final installment of Jeffrey Goldberg's series of foreign policy interviews with President Obama, a conversation that has spanned all eight years of his presidency. If each interview has served us a taste of what the most powerful man on earth was thinking at the time, then this final piece—an essay, not a transcript like the others—was the whole meal start to finish.

As the name of the essay suggests, Goldberg's piece lays out The Obama Doctrine, the organizing principle behind the momentous foreign policy of a man whose unlikely rise to the American presidency often overshadows his far more unlikely rise to the seat of Commander in Chief. Here's a man who went from being the Illinois State Senator to the commander of our armed forces in a mere four years—quite a remarkable feat.

No less remarkable a feat than Goldberg's essay itself, "The Obama Doctrine" isn't conjecture from historians poring through State of the Union transcripts decades later, but rather the words of a sitting president. The gravity of this essay cannot be overstated. In it, we see Obama reflect on specific decisions—not striking Assad, pivoting to Asia, intervening in Libya—only in order to make broader claims about his presidency, to situate himself historically among the liberal interventionists, the internationalists, the isolationists, and the realists.

Out of these schools, Obama says he is closest to the realists, believing that "we can't, at any given moment, relieve all the world's misery." He says, "We have to choose where we can make a real impact." That is why, he says, he stood quietly as Putin invaded Crimea in 2014, a core interest for Russia but hardly one for the United States. That is why he reneged on his 2012 promise to intervene in Syria after Assad deployed chemical weapons on his own people.

But not even the most sympathetic Obama supporter could go through Goldberg's piece and chalk his decisions these past eight years up to realism. Throughout the interview, one observes an insuperable level of disillusionment in our president. He laments the diplomatic ties and obligations he has to tolerate because of mere tradition—the misogynistic Saudis, the autocratic Turks, Bibi Netanyahu's exhausting condescension.

Obama also deplores the Western allies who ride on American coat tails, a claim that would be understandable if he at least took part of the blame for his missteps. In perhaps the most irritating line of the entire interview, Obama comments on the failure to stabilize Libya: "When I go back and I ask myself what went wrong, there's room for criticism, because I had more faith in the Europeans, given Libya's proximity, being invested in the follow-up."

"There's room for criticism because I had more faith in the Europeans"—no line better betrays this administration's gross misunderstanding of global power dynamics. A true realist—if we are to take Obama's self-identification seriously—understands that free-riding is a negligible price to pay for stability and is moreover an inevitable outcome of coalition diplomacy. If our president's sensibilities on fairness are enough cause to retreat, Russia and Iran are eager to eat the costs of free-riding if it means they could fill the lucrative power vacuum we would leave behind.

The most compelling case for the Obama Doctrine—which if not an offshoot of realism, is something more akin to "isolationism with drones and special-ops forces" as one critic calls it—was blown up this week in Brussels along with 34 civilians, in the deadliest act of terrorism in Belgian history. Obama claims that "ISIS is not an existential threat to the United States," rather "climate change is a potential existential threat to the entire world if we don't do something about it." This is jaded Obama at work—recklessly allowing his Weltschmerz to cloud his judgment, choosing more romantic, less controversial battles like climate change and the favorite cause of his first term, the "pivot to Asia."

This is not to discount Obama's likely genuine belief that climate change demands our attention more than terrorism. But at the root of this claim is not logic, but a fatigue of the Middle East and a yearning for something new. Obama explains to Goldberg about why he prefers to talk about Asia more than ISIS, "They are not thinking about how to kill Americans," he says. "What they're thinking about is 'How do I get a better education? How do I create something of value?'" This sounds like a man so lustful for hope that he's willing to radically skew his priorities.

Sample Essay 1, 2, 3 based on NEW SAT FORMULA

	INTRODUCTION
SAMPLE ESSAY 1	**In response to** "Islamic states and democracy", **writer** Idrees M. Kahloon **argues that** growing reliance on religion in the Muslim countries is an attempt to preserve and even consolidate power by the rulers of the countries. **His article** "Are democracy and constitutional Islam at odds?" **is effectively built upon through the contemplation of** major modern Islamic countries, compelling published indices, and historical background. **Idrees' overall purpose in writing this article appears to be to draw attention towards** not impeccable unification of religion and democracy, **in which sense his article is persuasive** to broad non-Muslim audience.
SAMPLE ESSAY 2	**In response to** "Artful advertising", **writer Lily K. Calcagnini argues that** although fashion belongs in museums, fashion tycoons such as Bernard Arnault, the CEO of LVMH or Miuccia Prada are mainly motivated by a selfish acts in founding fashion museum that affects the revenue of the clothing brand that bears their names. **Her article** "Fashion marketing moves from billboards to museum displays" **is effectively built upon through the contemplation of** her experience at the museum visit, the speculation hinged on the metropolitan's Costume institute's exhibition, and finally juxtaposition of the Valentino Garavani Virtual museum that she idealizes. **Lily's overall purpose in writing this article appears to be to draw attention towards** how fashion industry can be ideally converted into a widely accessible museum, instead of means to boost revenue of the fashion brands, **in which sense her article is persuasive** to her audience and let them evaluate the issue from critics' view.
SAMPLE ESSAY 3	**In response to** "hope and change, by any means necessary", **writer** Shubhankar Chhora **argues that** Obama's foreign policy during his presidency is not compliance with the pivotal role of U.S. against major global issues, dropping out chances to reform world orders. His article "Obama's disillusioned doctrine" **is effectively built upon through the contemplation of his overall performance in foreign policy. Chhora' overall purpose in writing this article appears to be to draw attention towards** extensive failure Obama created by not creating intended actions. **His article,** by employing the criticism crafted by other scholars and his stylistic elements with analytic tone, **is persuasive to his audience.**

BODY PARAGRAPH 1	
SAMPLE ESSAY 1	**In his introduction**, Idrees **starts with** the former convicted Egyptian President Mohamed Morsi, who, according to his critics, made "Egypt into an illiberal theocracy." **Idrees utilizes** this real-world case **to later support his argument by convincingly revealing the fact that** Egypt's next constitution was "shepherded" by the military. **Such a phrase forces the reader to question that** constitutional Islam could be fabricated based on secular-hypocrite motivation opposed to religious doctrine. **By delivering** this actual incidence, **the author leads the reader with more credence to his view.**
SAMPLE ESSAY 2	**In her introduction**, Lily **starts her analysis by questioning** the motivation of LVMH that it found a private museum of contemporary art in Paris. **She utilizes** a series of suspicion and discrepancies between what she observed at the museum and the motives of the CEO of LVMH, Bernard Arnault **to later support her argument by convincingly revealing the fact that** "the museum has begun to focus more on mounting provoking art shows…". **Such a phrase forces the reader to question that** the genuine purpose of founding the museum is only to boost the revenue. **By delivering** this actual incidence, **the author leads the reader with more credence to her view.** Like Sherlock Homs creates deductive reasoning at a crime scene, Lily invites her audience to unscramble the mystery. In front of the author, Arnault becomes an alleged criminal with a lack of alibi. Using such a tantalizing opening, the author's approach to this sort of investigative journalism lays out with full of reasoning and projection. Lily's investigation is furthered by her assertion that LVMH is losing its ground as newer fashion labels have begun to outmode its brand like Louis Vuitton in high fashion. She persuades the reader that this supposedly public museum at the heart of Paris can't be the museum that all people think. She fires up against Arnault that he has no other intention but revive the label of his company by founding a private museum.

BODY PARAGRAPH 1

SAMPLE

ESSAY 3

In his introduction, Shubhankar **utilizes his harsh criticism,** "Obama's rise to the seat of Commander in Chief is far more unlikely than the unlikelihood of his rise to the American presidency." **to later support his argument by convincingly revealing the fact that** " that is why he stood quietly as Putin invaded Crimea in 2014". **Such a phrase forces the reader**—especially those who support Obama-- **to question that** analytical reflections based upon evidential proof need to be examined. **By delivering** this actual incidence, **the author leads the reader with more credence to his view.**

Shubhankar reveals the comprehensive failure of Obama administration's foreign policy patched with mockery and accusation. "We have to choose where we can make a real impact.", after reneging to intervening Syria; "There's room for criticism because I had more faith in the Europeans", after failing to stabilizing Libya; and finally, "ISIS is not an existential threat to the United States," rather "climate change is". These quotes from president Obama persuade the reader to think that outcomes could have been better, than what he did.

To garner the audience attention from somewhat a heavy issue like Obama's foreign policy failure, Shubhankar employs various stylistic devise such as juxtaposition, irony, quotation. As an example, he categorizes a potential existential threat to the world and more romantic, less controversial battles like climate change or "pivot to Asia". Within this broad division he persuades the reader how illogical his doctrine has been; how irrational Obama has been in preceding and romanticizing grave world issues.

BODY PARAGRAPH 2

SAMPLE ESSAY 1

Followed by his analysis on what motivates rulers in some Muslim countries to adopt religious clauses in constitutions, **Idrees further solidifies his argument**, **bringing** academic researches **into his analytic argument.** He now elaborates the practical effects of constitutional declarations of Islam. **As an example**, Idrees **employs** "Islamic Constitutions Index" developed by Dawood I. Ahmed. The index scale shows interactions between religion and democracy among Muslim countries such as public morality, rights, legislation, and the judiciary. **By introducing** this published academic research, **Idrees's analysis gains competent evidence to back up his argument. Using** the stratified Muslim states' level of democracy, civil right protections, and how modestly or strongly coerce religious clause into their constitutions **ensure the reader to accept the facts that he presents without prejudice.** At the end of academic analysis, **he concludes that** "On average, constitutions with higher measures of Islamic provisions in their constitutions are associated with worse scores in The Economist Intelligence Unit's democracy index, Freedom House's civil liberties ratings, World Economic Forum's gender gap index, and the Pew Research Foundation's index of government restrictions on religion."

His reliance on the usage of academic and the officially released indices **is insightful in that** a subject like religion is very debatable and complicate issue that could easily loose support from either side or fall away from the author's original intentionn.

BODY PARAGRAPH 2

SAMPLE ESSAY 2	**Followed by her analysis on what motivates** CEO of LVMH, Bernard Arnault to found his private museum, **Lily further solidifies her argument** by **bringing Prada into her investigative analysis.** **Lily** starts with Prada's claim that "she endeavors her ambitions, not stemming from her need to invigorate her brands but from her confidence in her taste in fine art, which drove her to boasts her personal tastes in over 120,000 square feet of exhibition space. **By introducing** incredulous motivation of Prada, **Lily's analysis gains competent evidence to back up her argument.** "while The Fondazione Prada purports only to add to its foundress's empire, I'm interested to see how its opening affects the revenue of the clothing brand that bears her name." Her word choice clarifies the intention of Prada museum even without letting the reader to weigh credibility. **Her reliance on the insightful usage of word choice clarifies the intention of Prada museum even without letting the reader to weight the credibility.**
SAMPLE ESSAY 3	**Followed by his analysis on** president Obama's illogical approach to foreign policy from his fatigue and lighthearted naivety, Shubhankar **further solidifies his argument bringing** a quote from David Frum. "that all of us have disappointed Barack Obama" **into his analytic argument.** He, using several quotations from David Frum, reveals what Obama focused on his doctrine. Avoiding issues like "how to kill Americans" and adhering issues like "Asian education" leads the audience to take his side. From Shubhankar's eyes, Obama's denial of ISIS threat by underestimating terrorism, and exaggeration of climate change—which, the author believes, doesn't give us the same level of immediate threat as grave as the one we get from 9/11 or ISIS terrorism—establishes genuine doubt about Obama doctrine, if not a doubt about the president Obama himself. Shubhankar's view on Obama doctrine, although debatable, at least **gains competent evidence to back up his argument and** warns the reader who tends to proactively trust on Obama. The audience, after reading his article, will definitely open up the eyes to see Obama from a different angel **without prejudice. His reliance on the usage of quotes from** academic and rhetorical question **is insightful in that** it enlightens the reader to doubt about Obama Doctrine.

	BODY PARAGRAPH 3
SAMPLE ESSAY 1	**Finally, Idrees encourages the reader to view this less impressive correlation** between religion and democracy in Muslim countries **from a broader perspective**. He introduces Western nations' involvement in rewriting the Iraqi and Afghani constitutions. **He also warns that** between what constitutions prescribe and how the constitutional provisions are practiced in actual, day-to-day lives are quite different. **He further suggests that** we should factor in historical origins such as "repugnancy clauses" arose from the British rule of India. **His series of elaboration reflects** the matter of complexity, limitations of our understanding, and instability of foolproof analysis of this complicate issue. Although his resort to academic indices has its own merit to show credible percentages, figures and data, functional ethos in mainstream, we are unable to quantify Muslim states solely using the data or statistics, says the author. **In this regards, his judicious analytic inclusion of** historical view and other interpretation **requires us to evaluate this article without simple minded reaction.**
SAMPLE ESSAY 2	**Finally, Lily encourages the reader to view this less impressive correlation** between the private museum and fashion **from a broader perspective. She makes efficient use of** personal experience she had at the LVMH museum. **To rivet her audience's attention, she exemplifies** the collections: "four-figured price tag on a Chanel dress protected by the glass". Her comments on the collections express the symbolism of Arnault's resilience to preserve his revenue. **Her analytical strategy is definitely an appeal to emotion, forcing the audience to directly distinguish** Armault and Prada's false claims and the museum's single purpose in reality: a marketing tool. **She further suggests that** the reader to observe Valentino Garavani Virtual Museum in comparison to that of Prada or Arnault. She tells the reader Valentino's 3-D Virtual Museum allows anyone can explore over 5,000 dresses and many associate information. **This direct comparison by Lily suggests us to weigh why her analysis should be viewed with credence.** Her series of elaboration reflects the genuine discrepancies that she initially raises. **In this regards, her judicious analytic inclusion of** an ideal Valentino Garavani Virtual Museum **requires us to evaluate** how hollow Arnault and Prada's promises are.

BODY PARAGRAPH 3

SAMPLE
ESSAY 3

Finally, Shubahnakar **encourages the reader to view this less impressive Obama's foreign policy failure from a broader perspective.** In an effort to persuade his audience, he didn't seem to be afraid of the supporters of the incumbent president Obama. Rather, **He further suggests how pervasive likeminded analysis is among academics** with full of irony and sarcasm to bolster his argument. **His series of elaboration insightfully protects his argument mainly by articulating how critics believe about the issue.** When the issue is on-going, and therefore not enough evidential proof or data is available, probably an ultimate choice to get the reader's attention might be utilizing or touching the emotion with strong voice and word choice.

In this regards, his judicious analytic inclusion of Goldberg's interview and the quotes from David Frum requires us to evaluate this article without simple minded reaction.

CONCLUSION

SAMPLE ESSAY 1	**To sum up, idress's analytical skills that encompass** academic indices, historical aspects, and reasoning **greatly appeal to the reader. He cogently initiated his argument by revealing that** the religion in the Muslim countries is being exploited in an attempt to preserve and even consolidate power by the rulers of the countries. **He later leads the reader to view the issue with deeper insight. Therefore, it is clear that his argument is exceptionally persuasive in dealing with such a hotly debatable issue.**
SAMPLE ESSAY 2	**To sum up, Lily's investigative journal style article that encompasses her analytical skills, deductive reasoning, personal experience greatly appeal to the reader. By utilizing a juxtaposition between** the two dubious museums and an ideal museum, **she also cogently leads the reader to view the issue with deeper insight. Therefore, it is clear that her argument is exceptionally persuasive in dealing with such a debatable issue.**
SAMPLE ESSAY 3	**To sum up, Shubahnakar's article that encompasses his analytical skills, deductive reasoning,** Goldberg's interview, and a quote from David **greatly appeal to the reader. Shubahankar renders the audience to observe the genuine failure of Obama doctrine. In an effort to persuade his audience, Shubahnakar** didn't seem to be afraid of the supporters of the incumbent president Obama. **Rather, he sends a unqualified remarks with** full of irony and sarcasm **to bolster his analysis. His approach is quintessential because it insightfully protects his argument mainly by articulating how critics believe about the issue, in which he cogently leads the reader to view the issue with deeper insight. Therefore, it is clear that his argument is exceptionally persuasive in dealing with such a debatable issue.**

Ch. 1
Ch. 2
Ch. 3
Ch. 4
Ch. 5
Ch. 6
Ch. 7
Ch. 8
Ch. 9
Ch. 10

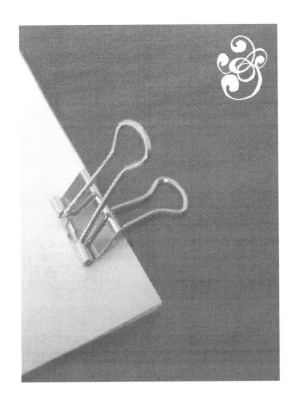

Chapter 6

Insightful
Vocabulary & Phrase
For Your Essay

Insightful Phrase for Essay

Most students find difficulty with the beginning sentence when they start writing an essay.

Please read the following vocabularies & phrases and practice to forumulate your own beginning sentence.

QEUSTION	The social part of life at a college or university is an important as the academic part.
ALTERNATE	The social part of life at a college contributes the pivotal function in maintaining a successful college life. With all due respect, it shall not alternate or substitute academic life.
PRACTICE	
QEUSTION	What's useful about the internet, and what's frustrating about the internet?
ARCHETYPE	The very archetype of modern technocracy and the way it operates can be represented by the groundbreaking invention, "internet". Internet, however, has always been debated about its impact to the society, analogously resembling the sward with both edges.
PRACTICE	
QEUSTION	Governments should publish the addresses of dangerous criminals who have been released from prison.
ANACHRONISM	Over the centuries, history has witnessed the exponential growth of industry and science. The backbone of society, judicial and legislative systems in modern society, however, seems to be somewhat stagnant in its development or even to be anachronic. The government has no right, and itself will further violate the law it intends to protect by disclosing criminal's (human being) very personal identity such as address to the public.
PRACTICE	
QEUSTION	Students should be allowed to share study information about take-home examinations on social networking sites such as facebook.

EFFICIENTLY ALLOCATE	To some degree, sharing information about the exam should efficiently allocate the quintessential knowledge about the school subjects. Since the main purpose of the exam is to measure the ability of a student's comprehension on a subject, study information should be freely transferred and exchanged among students regardless, but not excluding the SNS, of mode of transfer.
PRACTICE	
QEUSTION	At what point in a young person's life do you think adults should stop giving advice and helping with decision making?
ARTICULATE	By all means, adults should give the youth advice as often and articulately as possible. Empirical knowledge gained through decades of adult life always helps build ethical and reasoning capacity of the youth.
PRACTICE	
QEUSTION	Should students whose first language is not English and who are new to the U.S. school system not have to write English placements tests in order to get into college or university?
ATTEST	A series of evidence attest that the applicant's English placement test scores do not reflect the student's overall scholastic aptitude in college.
PRACTICE	
QEUSTION	Should unacceptable web surfing in the workplace be a reason to fire someone from his or her job?
AGGRAVATE	Surfing the websites that contain sexual or anti-social contents in a workplace does not help alleviate tension or stress built-up at work, but only aggravate work ethos.
PRACTICE	
QEUSTION	Is being a young person today more difficult than it was 30 years ago?
CARCINOGENIC	When the parents of children 30 years ago cried over the carcinogenic effects of rock and roll music and Heavy metal lyrics, they could at least afford the moderate city living. Young people today concern less about such intrinsic or moral issues. All they care about is whether they could afford the bills coming up next week for rentals, cars, and insurance.

PRACTICE	
QEUSTION	Patients should have the right to refuse life-saving medical treatment
CRUX OF THE MATTER	The issue whether patients should demand their rights to discontinue life supporting treatment or be left with the medical practitioner's authority has long been hotly debated. The crux of the matter is neither ethical nor judicial. The intrinsic nature of this issue resides in financial affordability of the patients.
PRACTICE	
QEUSTION	Should manufacturers of genetically modified foods be required to label their products?
CAPITALISM	In a view from Capitalism, the manufactured goods serve its greatest purpose when, and only when it generates the highest yield with the lowest resources input. When the purpose is good for the majority, some minor known or not yet fully proven flaws must be sacrificed and compromised. Genetic food is one of the scapegoats that has been persistently scrutinized for its hazardous impact to human health. With all due respect, labeling genetic products must be judiciously examined.
PRACTICE	
QEUSTION	Tips should be included in the bill for all service oriented industries.
CORROSIVE	One of the most corrosive traditions in all service oriented industries is demanding tips from customers, who are troubled to consider to pay tips when the service rendered is opposite from their expectation. Giving no tips, or at least leave it as a private decision will drop the prices that means more demand for goods and services.
PRACTICE	
QEUSTION	Should smoking on stage during an artistic performance be banned?
CONSOLIDATE	The go't censorship has always confronted dilemma. So sensitive is the issue of banning on the artistic expression and freedom that the gov't has given in too much freedom to the public. It is evident that individual's perception should be secured and respected. While government loosens its censorship, it, at the very same degree, consolidates antisocial and deleterious impact. Therefore, smoking or drinking during the art performance should be censored by the government.

PRACTICE	
QEUSTION	Is creativity needed more than ever in the world today?
COMPLETELY NULLIFY	The real threat in modern education system is not the lack of resources, but the opposite—too many subjects to teach that mainly focus on science, math, and foreign language, while completely nullifying art-related subjects that require creativity. Students put artistic creativity in their brains would spread their knowledge through other subjects.
QEUSTION	Does being ethical make it hard to be successful?
A KEY OBJECTIVE	In this hyper-competitive business world, being ethical may appear to be an extraordinary thing. With all due respect, a key objective in business is maintaining loyalty, a loyalty with the clients, a loyalty with employees. Ethical values cannot be traded for profit or success at any rate.
PRACTICE	
QEUSTION	Is it sometimes necessary to be impolite?
ORTHODOX	In an orthodox view of the world, being polite is likely to gain more favorable response. However, we might need to sand down the edges of human relations—though it might appear to be impolite—in an effort to repair and improve relations.
PRACTICE	
QEUSTION	Should we limit our use of the term "courage" to acts in which people risk their own well-being for the sake of others or to uphold a value?
OSTRACIZE	The term "courage" has been essentially unchallenged from business world, politics, and history. If someone's success was ground on his courage, society has accepted it and abandoned means and process. However, if such a courageous act is based on the delivery of personal prosperity and craving for personal honor while attenuating others chance, such a courageous act must be ostracized from our society.
PRACTICE	

QEUSTION	Does planning interfere with creativity?
QUINTESSEN-TIAL	Although two quintessential values: planning and creativity may resist each other to form and maintain success, in intellectual circles, these values make each other useful and eventually transcend one another. For instance, a government working with full-spectrum of planning tries its best to forge a creative society, a religiously, politically, and culturally creative but unified society.
PRACTICE	
QEUSTION	Do highly accomplished people achieve more than others mainly because they expect more of themselves?
PRACTICE	
QEUSTION	Should people change their decisions when circumstances change, or is it best for them to stick with their original decisions?
MALIGNANT	We have learned that anyone willingness to overthrow the status quo or change his decision when circumstances change is a malignant defector whom should not be trusted. However, such a conservative skepticism should be guarded in modern technocratic society, where our trends are moving in a nanosecond.
PRACTICE	
QEUSTION	Is persistence more important than ability in determining a person's success?
PARADIGM SHIFT	The modern system—liberal, democratic, capitalist—has made a paradigm shift when it comes to wealth. No more valued is one's innate ability or family background. Anyone accepts persistence can grasp chance in a closer proximity.
PRACTICE	
QEUSTION	Is acting an essential part of everyday life?
PIVOTAL	By all means, to absorb human relation's fractious nature, acting is a pivotal part of our lives.
PRACTICE	

 Ch. 1
 Ch. 2
 Ch. 3
 Ch. 4
 Ch. 5
 Ch. 6
Ch. 7
 Ch. 8
 Ch. 9
 Ch. 10

QEUSTION	Do you support human cloning?
REPLICATE	Human cloning—in ultimate technological progress—might be realized, man, however, does not have the potential to replicate the nature of human being.
PRACTICE	
QEUSTION	Is compromise always the best way to resolve a conflict?
RAMIFICATIONS	When there is not yet defining resolution to conflict available, preventing catastrophic ramifications is the primary goal. In that sense, compromise should not be looked as a passive or retreat, but as an active and progressive solution.
PRACTICE	
QEUSTION	Are decisions made quickly just as good as decisions made slowly and carefully?
POLARIZE	In society, there are groups of people less prominent but still culturally significant such as ethnic minorities, elders, or disabled people. Seeking a policy to reconcile their needs not only reduces polarization in society, but also consolidates unity.
PRACTICE	
QEUSTION	Can a group of people function effectively without someone being in charge?
INVETERATE	The inveterate problem, addressed the city mayor, in our society is that it is governed by sociopath politician, crooked police officers, and blood-sucking businessmen.
PRACTICE	
QEUSTION	Is capitalism the role model of modern society?
STARK CONTRAST	The stark contrast is seen at the downtown Vancouver, where druggies and prostitutes refuge their tormented lives, while the riches live on absolutely unapproachable pinnacle in uptown Vancouver. From this socioeconomic division emerges the western capitalism.
PRACTICE	

QEUSTION	Is modern technology contributing better lives ?
SUBSTANTIAL	The substantial role of SNS itemizes all the illegal activities available among youth within a mouse-click away: marijuana trafficking, prostitute, gun trafficking, unionized bullying.
PRACTICE	
QEUSTION	Is the modern society completely free from gender inequality?
STIGMATIZE	For women living in Islamic countries, searching for an egalitarian society seems impossibly far off. Women are innately stigmatized to expect only reasonable liberty, given absolutely no chance to elevate their social position.
PRACTICE	
QEUSTION	What is the benefit of modern technology?
TRANSIENT	From the modern medical standards, which have extended human life-expectancy up to 80 years in some western countries, men in 1500's with their life-expectancy at around 40s lived almost transient life.
PRACTICE	
QEUSTION	Are we enjoying better and more egalitarian society?
DISRUPT / RESTORE STATUS QUO	In most cases status quo favors ruling groups in societies. From their view, creative progress is understood as bad as disruption of status quo.
PRACTICE	
QEUSTION	Does being moral hinder the success?
UNDERPINNING	Ethics is the crux of underpinning what man should continue to strive. However, oddly enough, people forget about morality of successful figures, and their immorality is often forgiven because of their success.
PRACTICE	

QEUSTION	Does being moral hinder the success?
	Aforementioned analysis helps us to view that an immensely wealthy and privileged person, accustomed to having his way, is often forgiven even when he violates every moral in society.
PRACTICE	
They Are Human, With Human Flaws And Weaknesses	Both the employer and the claimant are not completely good or evil. They are human, with human flaws and weaknesses
PRACTICE	
Underpinning Their Society...	It is how these flawed characters influence and are influenced by the major themes **underpinning their society.**
PRACTICE	
During His Closing Arguments	During his closing arguments the author explicitly acknowledges the ignorance blinding people's minds and hearts.
PRACTICE	
The Most Important Theme Of The Story Remains The Notion Of	**The most important theme of the story remains the notion** of ignorance in all of its forms.
As Long As	Adolph Hitler proclaimed that **as long as the ends are positive for everyone, means and moral for success should be temporized**
PRACTICE	
As Revealed On The Above Analysis,	As revealed on the above analysis, the narcissism at the material oriented hierarchic society tends to enervate the development of the healthy society.
PRACTICE	
on the contrary,	on the contrary, we, sometimes, wonder if human controls the computer or computer does.
PRACTICE	

Though It May Sound Paradoxical,	**Though it may sound paradoxical**, only by strictly controlling freedom, absolute freedom can be secured.
PRACTICE	
The Surest Way To Guarantee	**The surest way to guarantee** freedom is to reduce chaos. Discipline never debilitates our freedom, but only makes stronger.
PRACTICE	
QUESTION	Do people have to pay attention to mistakes in order to make progress?
In Ideal World, We Might See	**In ideal world, we might see** those who succeed without willingness to fail. Understanding problems or responsibility would not necessarily trouble their success-oriented minds.
PRACTICE	
Although .... Is Not Something To Appreciate	**Although** making mistakes **is not something to appreciate,** one who does not learn from mistakes will never learn complexity and diversity of life. Imperfection is just a part of progress to perfection.
PRACTICE	
QUESTION	Is the society advancing for the better?
Whether It Is Good Or Bad	Should we have been grateful if our ancestors prefer peace, quiet, and frugality, instead of war, industrialism, capitalism? Unfortunately, the development of modern industry thrived under the turmoil of class revolution, shadow of war weaponry development, and greedy entrepreneur's capitalism mindset. **Whether it is good or bad,** society knows no bound of progress, all the negative effects, along with some positive ones, influence and educate us. Brain washed children are tacitly educated, and then they assimilate themselves into abnormal states such as same sex marriage, rampant drug usage, cooperative bullying at school. Society is definitely advancing for better materialistically, but is defiantly retrogressing for worse morally.
PRACTICE	

Ch. 1
Ch. 2
Ch. 3
Ch. 4
Ch. 5
Ch. 6
Ch. 7
Ch. 8
Ch. 9
Ch. 10

While ..., We Indeed See...	**While** tremendous unforeseen part of someone or something often betrays us, **we indeed see** many more people who try to balance external and
PRACTICE	
QUESTION	is listening criticism eventually benefit us?
IS Never Less Than	Being at the center of criticism **is never less than** taking awful taste of medicine.
PRACTICE	
While... Proportionately Ameliorates	**While** harsh criticism sometimes makes us hard to breathe, **we can easily estimate that** healthy criticism **proportionately ameliorates** our self-esteem later.
PRACTICE	
QUESTION	Is it better for people to acknowledge who they are, or should we always struggle to better ourselves?
Of All The Qualities Man Should Resemble,... Is The Greatest Virtue.	**Of all the qualities man should resemble,** striving to enhance the status quo **is the greatest virtue.**
PRACTICE	
Although Some May Argue That ... Is What Motivates Us To Progress	**Although** some **may argue** that chasing insatiable earthly desire lasts only as long as one's life, pursuing improvement at every chance **is what motivates us to progress**
PRACTICE	
QUESTION	Can common sense be trusted and accepted, or should it be questioned?
Within The Conventional Value	**Within the conventional value** that establishes and maintains successful society, commonly accepted principles often exert more power than
PRACTICE	
Although ..., If Not...	**Although** some, especially younger generations, may find only the iconoclastic spirit promotes society, common sense has weathered decades, **if not centuries**, of test and trial. **Thus, it gives steadfast conviction** to accept and follow years to come.

A Time Worn Cliché	**A time worn cliché** "you can't judge a book by its cover" enlightens us to avoid external appearance
PRACTICE	
We Are Often Awaken By The Fact That .... Does Not Exactly Parallel With	**We are often awaken by the fact that** the discovery of one's external beauty **does not exactly parallel with** his or her internal one.
PRACTICE	

QUESTION	When some people win, must others lose, or are there situations in which everyone wins?
Imagine...	**Imagine** the Olympic podium, on which three competitors wear three gold medals simultaneously, victoriously waving their hands. Karl Marx argued that capitalism will inevitably produce internal tensions which will lead to its destruction. He asserted it is as destructive as feudalism and believed communism will in turn, replace capitalism which leads society a classless, pure free nations. His theory, however, ended with the debacle of the former Soviet Union by proving outright impracticality of his theory.
PRACTICE	
QUESTION	Should people let their feelings guide them when they make important decisions?
Ethos, Pathos, Logos ...	Aristotle taught that the ability to make important decision comes when the fact appeals to his or her group in three different areas: **ethos (ethical appeals), pathos (emotional appeals), and logos (logical appeals).**.
PRACTICE	
···Explicitly Suggest That	The above described historical figures' flaws **explicitly suggest that** (there is a reason to tolerate flaws of great figures)
PRACTICE	

Ch. 1 Ch. 2 Ch. 3 Ch. 4 Ch. 5 Ch. 6 **Ch. 7** Ch. 8 Ch. 9 Ch. 10

Hence,...	With the advent of industrialism, modern science placed human's unique logical nature to the highest point in making idealistic decision. **Although scientific nature tends to localize logic as the highest virtue,** great classic artists enlightened us, not by logic, but by emotion. Hence, **there is nothing mystical about** human feelings' integral role in making important decision
PRACTICE	
QUESTION	Is listening criticism eventually benefit us?
Rarely Ever Has...	**Rarely ever has** any president in U.S. history escaped from the media criticism during his presidency. Roosevelt once commented that "media watchdog is bitter medicine for reducing government authoritarianism and enhancing true democracy. "
PRACTICE	
Under The Name Of...	While critical view from others is valuable element for self-introspection that can lead to eventual amelioration, Personal character defamation **under the name of** critical advice contributes nothing, rather worse off the relations.
PRACTICE	
QUESTION	The flaws of the heroic people benefit us
The Theme ...Is Not Limited To ...; We See This Immutable Principle Illustrated	**The theme** (the flaws of the heroic people benefit us)**is not limited to literary examples; we see this immutable principle illustrated throughout history, too.** Consider (World War II) if you will
PRACTICE	
···Had Far Reaching Implications... Granted That...	The effects of WWII had **far reaching implications for** the international community. Many millions of lives had been lost as a result of war. The ghosts of the world wars lived for another half century in the form of the Cold War between the United States and Soviet Union. While WWII begot the main culprit Adolf Hitler, the world also made heroes such as Theodor Roosevelt and Winston Churchill. Confronting numerous oppositions and sacrificing lives, these two heroes rebuilt peace and ended the Great War. **Granted that** some of their personal and strategic flaws might have existed, radical dictatorship, nationalism, ever widen gap between the rich and the poor would not have been materialized.

In His Famous Work, "The Prince",	In his famous work, "the Prince", Machiavelli wrote that a ruler must use any methods available to him to maintain stability, for even though some methods might seem abusive and inexorable. Flaws (cruelty), in reality benefit the people because the highest virtue of the ruler exactly the parallels with what the people ask for: stability. True, ethics are questionable, but if looking at the ends is so favorable to the mass, it would be futile to look at it otherwise. Had the prince not betrayed his cruelty, which might seem flaws to the mass, people would not have sacrificed their safety. This example confirms that flaws of the people we admire indeed benefit people
PRACTICE	
Contrary To The Expectation,	contrary to the expectation, individuals who realized their own goals become too powerful in their favorable conditions, by which they are fettered,
PRACTICE	
As Seen On The Above Analysis,	As seen on the above analysis, despite their many flaws, however, widely respected people can be paradigmatic guidance, allowing us to compare between ultimate success and ultimate downfall.
PRACTICE	
It Must Be Judiciously Evaluated	but, in order to implement its cardinal value of the past and to effectively set a paradigm for the future, it must be judiciously evaluated.
PRACTICE	
From This Perspective,	From this perspective-- commonly accepted sense will profoundly and positively affect the quality of society.
PRACTICE	
Ultimately,	Ultimately, William Golding, reflecting (Ralph's despotism and natural human barbarianism,) proposed that it is (the material world that is real and that our ideas of it are consequences, not causes, of the world.)
PRACTICE	

The Main Theme Of Hamlet Finds That...	The main theme of Hamlet finds that the destruction wrought when ambition goes unchecked by moral constraints
PRACTICE	
The Problem, The Play Suggests, Is That	The problem, the play suggests, is that once one decides to use violence to further one's quest for power, it is difficult to stop.
PRACTICE	
It Is Always Tempting To	It is always tempting to use violent means to protect peace.
PRACTICE	
Arguably, Lee Traces The Root Of	Arguably, Lee traces the root of chaos and evil to inveterate prejudice. While the evil characters are just as violent and prone to evil as white people, the aggression of the united town folks is more striking because it goes against prevailing expectations of small rustic town. Lee certainly shows that spectators can be as cruel as the main culprit.
PRACTICE	
··· Symbolizes...	Greed is everywhere in the Lord of the flies. Greed symbolizes the guilt that sits like a permanent stain on the consciences of boys, one that hounds them to the grave.
Our Initial Impression Is Of... The Perspective Is Complicated, However,	Our initial impression is of greed. The perspective is complicated, however, once we see Donald. J. Trump interacts with the socially deprived class.
PRACTICE	
···Offers No Easy Answers.	The election result offers no easy answers.
PRACTICE	

As Long As Social Constraints Deny	As long as social constraints deny racial equality, the current judicial methods--that is, manipulated and bias—will further support white-dominated society.
The Author Dismantles ... to Reveal	**The author dismantles** the photo of eight-year-old girl **to reveal** an underpinning rotten bigotry, filled with lies of bullying.
PRACTICE	
QUESTION	Has modern day's inundation of information made our lives more difficult?
Analogous To	Current internet network organization **can be analogous to** myriad of infinitesimal neural blood vessel in human body.
PRACTICE	
Hardly Is There Any	**Hardly is there any** individual or business that has not been touched by internet: from elementary student to some resident living in one of the most remote country in the world.
PRACTICE	
Although It Is Evident That... Should Never Be Oversighted.	**Although it is evident that** overflowing of information has expanded the periphery of our daily living, Side-effect of unfiltered information that affects human's fundamental psyche and its detrimental social impact at large **should never be oversighted.**
QUESTION	Do people need discipline to achieve freedom?
In Order To	Absolute state of freedom must be the most glamorous idea to everyone. **In order to** gain such a freedom, human employed war to destroy any external influence, taking away the other side's freedom.
PRACTICE	

Ch. 1　Ch. 2　Ch. 3　Ch. 4　Ch. 5　Ch. 6　Ch. 7　Ch. 8　Ch. 9　Ch. 10

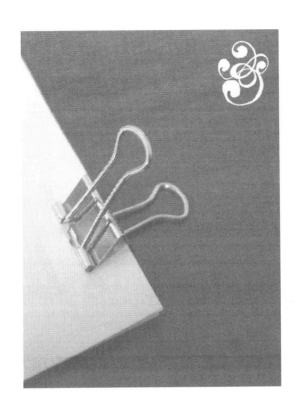

Chapter 8

ESSAY FORMAT FOR
ACT / TOEFL / IELTS

ESSAY FORMAT FOR ACT / TOEFL / IELTS

In this chapter we will review how we can utilize format for other standardized tests such as ACT/ Toefl / Ielts.

Please review the following format, and practice until you are familiar with your own formula to create your own essay that can be applicable on your tests.

Just keep in mind, the purpose of format is to aid your essay writing mechanically regardless of the topic given on the test. Thus, adhering to the format should not be adjusted frequently. Again, the standardized tests do not measure students' literary skills, but rather focuses on critical and analytical skills, which can be fashioned through repeated practice using the similar formation.

ACT/ TOEFL / IETLS ESSAY FORMAT

	Introduction Paragraph
TOPIC OPPOSITE OPINION	A lot of controversy exists over whether ... When it comes to ... There is no question that … It is often said that ... It goes without saying that… Without a doubt, ...
REASONING	In particular, Indeed,
CONCESSION	Although, / However, / With all due respect, / Granted that / In spite of / While...
THESIS	
	Body Paragraph 1
TOPIC BACKGROUND	To begin with, ...
REASONING	To illustrate, ….
CONCLUSION	
	Body Paragraph 2
TOPIC PROBLEM	In addition,
REASONING	

Body Paragraph 3	
TOPIC SOULUTION	
REASONING	To illustrate, ….
Conclusion	
RESTATEMENT OF THE THESIS	
THE FUTURE PREDICTION	

Ch. 1
Ch. 2
Ch. 3
Ch. 4
Ch. 5
Ch. 6
Ch. 7
Ch. 8
Ch. 9
Ch. 10

THE EXAMPLE ESSAY 1 FOR TOEFL AND IELTS

ASSIGNMENT: Should the secondary school include art education ?

INTRODUCTION PARAGRAPH	
OPPOSITE OPINION	<u>***When* thinking of**</u> Secondary school subjects over the past few decades, pundits and academic administrators have pursued their endeavors on a few major subjects such as math, science, and foreign languages, while suffocating art education nearly to death.
SUPPORTING DETAIL	Such an atmosphere has also been fortified by politicians and industries, where tax money spending could be transparently reflected on legislation and where skilled labor could be harnessed immediately in industries. Many parents naively believed that focusing on major school subjects will make their children's lives better.
CONCESSION & THESIS	**With all due respect,** fostering children by destroying art subjects will create dysfunctional intelligence.
BODY PARAGRAPH 1	
BACKGROUND INFORMATON & THE CURRENT SITUATION	**To begin with,** school prioritizes major subjects that can directly affect to college entrance tests. To respond high demands on major subjects, many schools are competing one another to introduce the AP or IB courses heavily focusing on science, math, and language courses in their regular lesson plans. Once major courses are set forth by the decision of the school board, opinions from the students may not be heard. **For instance,** many art students won't even find a legitimate chance to take art honor courses or AP courses because there is simply no such a course exists. Art students, the end-users, simply have no power to alter the school administration's decision to have art courses in school.

BODY PARAGRAPH 2

PROBLEM & MAJOR CONCERNS	Post-industrial revolution required in-depth knowledge of science, math, and foreign language skills from the workers. As we are entering technocratic era, **on the other hand,** more and more industries are focusing not on durability or functionality of the consumer products anymore, but on the design that requires sensual techniques. Without getting a proper art education from school, students will simply unable to receive art education that can be officially recognized from the industries and also won't attain skills that industries require. Under the current school education system, it would be overwhelming to implement high costs art studio as most of the budget is being allocated to major school subjects to hire teachers, materials, and facilities. **Indeed,** students' voices rarely get much traction in school politics, **although** the administration itself knows that the current education supports unbalanced coursework system. What we do get is a pervasive angst among art students and their parents. While non-art majoring students often don't realize how good they have it, art majoring students seem not to realize how terribly they are being treated.

BODY PARAGRAPH 3

SOLUTIONS & PREDICTION	**It is not to say that** individual secondary school should manage all the art courses, install an expensive studio, and hire specialty instructors, the luxuries most schools simply can't afford. **Despite of the current constrains, however, there are ways to improve** art education. Each school district can establish a communal art studio, where every school within the district can share the studio depending on demands. By doing so. Individual school does not have to feel anxiety to have its own art studio or art instructors, and costly materials. The parents can manage their financial stress by not sending their artistically talented kids to a luxurious private art schools. The art students do not have to panic for their penchant for arts instead of science.

CONCLUSION	
RESTATMENT OF THE THESIS (if applicable, the future prediction)	Both school administrators and the politicians have to take stands on the art education to secondary school students. **Moreover,** industries need it—desperately. Once the mandatory art education regulation is established, there should be many ways to foster our children to art competitive generation.

ESSAY PRACITCE

Before you begin writing your essay based on the formula, please read the following criteria and try to include all the criteria on your essay.

THE CRITERIA FOR HIGH SCORE ESSAY	YES OR NO?
Consistently excellent, with at most a few minor errors.	YES / NO
Takes a clear position on the topic and uses insightful relevant examples to back it up.	YES/ NO
Shows strong overall organization and paragraph development.	YES/ NO
Demonstrates a superior command of language, as shown by varied sentence structure and word choice.	YES/ NO
Two ~ Three examples listed in paragraph 1	YES/ NO
Topic sentence for example in paragraph 2.	YES/ NO
3–4 development sentences to support paragraph 2's example.	YES/ NO
Topic sentence for example in paragraph 3.	YES/ NO
3–4 development sentences to support paragraph 3's example.	YES/ NO
Conclusion paragraph contains rephrased thesis statement.	YES/ NO
About 350~550 words in total.	YES/ NO

ESSAY PRCTICE FOR TOEFL AND IELTS

INTRODUCTION PARAGRAPH	
OPPOSITE OPINION	
SUPPORTING DETAIL	
CONCESSION & THESIS	
BODY PARAGRAPH 1	
BACKGROUND INFORMATON & THE CURRENT SITUATION	

BODY PARAGRAPH 2

PROBLEM & MAJOR CONCERNS	

BODY PARAGRAPH 3

SOLUTIONS & PREDICTION	

Ch. 1
Ch. 2
Ch. 3
Ch. 4
Ch. 5
Ch. 6
Ch. 7
Ch. 8
Ch. 9
Ch. 10

CONCLUSION	
RESTATMENT OF THE THESIS (if applicable, the future prediction)	

SAN'S NEW SAT ESSAY

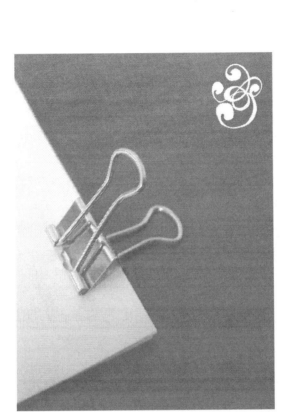

Chapter 9

QUOTATIONS FOR YOUR INSIGHTFUL INTRODUCTION & CONCLUSION

QUOTATIONS FOR YOUR INSIGHTFUL INTRODUCTION & CONCLUSION PARAGRAPHS

Starting or ending your essay using an insightful quotation can back up your thesis even stronger. The reason is simple. Although your thesis might seem to be biased, weak in evidence, or lack of persuasion, it is virtually impossible for the reader to go against a meaningful quotation from a historic figure's speech. If you use it wisely—only once in your entire essay—your introduction or conclusion should look impeccable—at least in that area. I think it is o.k. not to remember exactly who said your quotation. Memorizing difficult authors' names, not to mention many quotations with different categories, does not have to be precise—at least during the test. History will forgive you, the already dead heroes will be generous, and the most of all, the grader won't remember who exactly said the quotation that you are referring to your essay.

 Ch. 1
 Ch. 2
 Ch. 3
 Ch. 4
 Ch. 5
 Ch. 6
 Ch. 7
 Ch. 8
 Ch. 9
 Ch. 10

Essay Topics Related With

Happiness / Materialism / Social Accomplishment / Way Of Life / Ethics

	The German philosopher Arthur Schopenhauer (1788-1860) is well known for his pessimism. He did not believe in real happiness. In his view, the best person can achieve is to reduce misery. Arthur Schopenhauer
	The man who goes up in a balloon does not feel as if he were ascending; he only sees the earth sinking deeper below him. Arthur Schopenhauer
	Man is never happy, but spends his whole life in striving after something which he thinks will make him so. Arthur Schopenhauer
	Happiness belongs to those who are sufficient unto themselves. For all external sources of happiness and pleasure are, by their very nature, highly uncertain, precarious, ephemeral and subject to change. Arthur Schopenhauer
	With people of only moderate ability is mere honesty; but with those who possess great talent it is hypocrisy. Arthur Schopenhauer
	After your death you will be what you were before your birth. Arthur Schopenhauer
	Will power is to the mind like a strong blind man who carries on his shoulders a lame man who can see. Arthur Schopenhauer
	Wealth is like sea water; the more we drink, the thirstier we become; and the same is true of fame. Arthur Schopenhauer
	Living in a constant chase after gain compels people to expand their spirit to the point of exhaustion. Friedrich Nietzsche
	We think too much and feel too little. Charlie Chaplin
	Life is a tragedy when seen in close-up, but a comedy in long-shot. – Charlie Chaplin
	The basic essential of a great actor is that he loves himself in acting. – Charlie Chaplin
	The saddest thing I can imagine is to get used to luxury –Charlie Chaplin

Essay Topics Related With Art, Culture, Science

1	Many books serve merely to show how many ways there are of being wrong, and how far astray you yourself would go if you followed their guidance. You should read only when your own thought dry up -Arthur Schopenhauer
2	It is only in the microscope that our life looks so big. It is an indivisible point, drawn out and magnified by the powerful lenses of Time and Space. -Arthur Schopenhauer
3	Every man takes the limits of his own vision for the limits of the world. -Arthur Schopenhauer
4	To art, we, humans are so miserable, weak and invisible. The more we accomplish ourselves, the greater the nature of art can we observe. -Arthur Schopenhauer

Essay Topics Related With Family, Community, Societal Interaction

5	Too many people let others stand in their way and don't go back for one more try. -Immanuel Kant
6	Whosoever desires constant success must change his conduct with the times. - Niccolo Machiavelli
7	If an injury has to be done to a man it should be so severe that his vengeance need not be feared. -Niccolo Machiavelli
8	It is better to be feared than loved, if you cannot be both.—Niccolo Machiavelli
9	Men in general judge more by the sense of sight than by the sense of touch, because everyone can see, but only a few can test by feeling. Everyone sees what you seem to be, few know what you really are, and those few do not dare to take a stand against the general opinion. –Niccolo Machiavelli.
10	There is no avoiding war, it can only be postponed to the advantage of others.- Adolf Hitler
11	The masses are far more likely to believe a big lie than several small ones. Adolf Hitler
12	A person is far more likely to appear to have sound character because he persistently follows his temperament than because he persistently follows his principles. Friedrich Nietzsche

13	There are no facts, only interpretations. Friedrich Nietzsche
14	Those who were seen dancing were thought to be insane by those who could not hear the music. -Friedrich Nietzsche
15	He who fights with monsters might take care lest he thereby become a monster. -Friedrich Nietzsche

Essay Topics Related With Success, Job, Economy

16	To stay ahead, you must have your next idea waiting in the wings. Immanuel Kant
17	He who blinded by ambition, raises himself to a position whence he cannot mount higher, must thereafter fall with the greatest loss. –Niccolo Machiavelli
18	There is nothing so useless as doing efficiently that which should not be done at all. -Peter Drucker
19	There is the risk you cannot afford to take, there is risk you cannot afford not to take. -Peter Drucker
20	Believe me! The secret of reaping the greatest fruitfulness and the greatest enjoyment from life is to live dangerously. -Friedrich Nietzsche
21	The leaders who work most effectively, it seems to me, never say "I", and that's not because they have trained themselves not to say "I". They don't think "I", they think "we", they think team." They understand their job to be to make the team function. They accept responsibility and don't sidestep it. This is what creates trust, what enables you to get the task done." –Peter Drucker
22	How can we overcome the resistance to innovation that plagues most organization? –Peter Drucker
	<u>Martin Luther King, Jr.</u> Darkness cannot drive out darkness; only light can do that. Hate cannot drive out hate; only love can do that. Human progress is neither automatic nor inevitable... Every step toward the goal of justice requires sacrifice, suffering, and struggle; the tireless exertions and passionate concern of dedicated individuals.

Essay Format Using The Quotation To Support Your Thesis

Does being ethical interfere with success?

INTRODUCTION PARAGRAH

Without a doubt, if you want to succeed, you have to think like a billionaire.
I can hardly imagine that ethical duty, from the view of financially successful figures, can be counted as an integral premise for success.
With all due respect, and although being ethical may not even remotely affect success in this capitalism-indulged society, lasting success should base its foundation on ethical value.
Compelling example can be found in the recent case of the U.S. Presidential nominee and the history.

BODY PARAGRAPH 1

An example that proves that (being ethical should be the premise of success) **can be found in the case of** Mr. Donald. J. Trump, the Republican presidential nominee. **Mr. Don**ald J. Trump, during the race, **used** his financial success to seduce the public.
In a recent media revelation, the 2005 "Access Hollywood", in which Trump said "I don't even wait. And when you're a star, they let you do it, you can do anything…grab them by the women's genitals." Mr. Trump showed how he acted like, or to be frank, lower than a hangingfly. (A hangingfly is a type of insect that catches other smaller insects, then uses it to seduce a passing female. While she dines on his nuptial gift, he gets to mate with her.) As the film explicitly showed, Mr. Trump has been using his inherited wealth to seduce naïve voters, especially those in working class desiring to be rich like Mr. Trump.

On the contrary, almost all self-made successful figures display a single-minded determination to impose their vison on the world—though many times seem unreasonable, and bordering on lunacy, they crave for success built upon the scratch. Therefore, they appreciate the value of success, which is unthinkable from a recent presidential candidate in U.S as a member of the lucky sperm club. Among many factors, these self-made figures define morals as it be fit into the business world to preserve what they have created within it.

Had Mr. Trump learned his path to success from the scratch, he would have realized—and been approved by others—that ethical values also affect success. Some say that it is unfair to compare Mr. Trump to dog. They are right. Dog are awesome.

BODY PARAGRAPH 2

The theme that (ethics must be the premise of success) **is also illustrated in history."**
We all know that Galileo Galilei redirected our view on world, from geocentricism to helliocentricism. Behind his contributions to astronomy, and modern science at large though, the excruciating accusation from the public and the church are not much discussed. He risked his own life to maintain his discovery. Considering the times he lived when the Christianity dominated the culture, politics, and people's daily living, having a conflict with the church meant to be political death sentence.
His helliocentricism required a tremendous determination, which ground upon ethical duty as a scientist.
Of course, this is not to say that in times, we all should sacrifice everything we have to preserve ethics. What we should argue is that in the absence of ethical judgment, human can turn into a vicious animal without reasoning.

CONCLUSION

As Friedrich Nietzsche once wrote, "He who fights with monsters might take care lest he thereby become a monster." Reveals how success or desire unchecked by morals can destroy oneself

SAN'S NEW SAT ESSAY

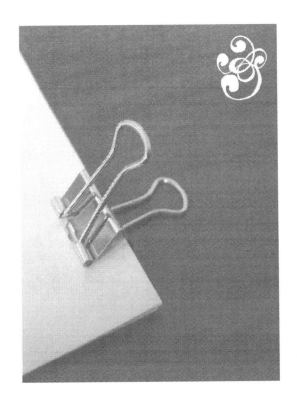

Chapter 10

Self Editing Practice

Self Editing Practice

Direction: each question is composed of three different levels of difficulties: Harder level question does not show the error in the sentence; Middle level question underlines the error, so you can fix it; Basic level question gives you the four selections for you to choose the right answer just like the one that appears on the actual SAT question.

Try harder level first by covering up the middle and basic level questions using a piece of paper. If you are unable to find the error from the hard level, move on to the middle level, or to the basic level for practice.

Ch. 1

Ch. 2

Ch. 3

Ch. 4

Ch. 5

Ch. 6

Ch. 7

Ch. 8

Ch. 9

Ch. 10

Harder Question 1	For decades the paleontologists had assumed that the Ice Age killed the dinosaurs, and their views changed quickly where the most massive meteorite crater was found in Yucatan.
Middle Question 1	For decades the paleontologists had assumed that the Ice Age killed the dinosaurs, <u>and their views changed quickly where</u> the most massive meteorite crater was found in Yucatan.
Basic Question 1	For decades the paleontologists had assumed that the Ice Age killed the dinosaurs, <u>and their views changed quickly where</u> the most massive meteorite crater was found in Yucatan. A) NO CHANGE B) since their views changed quickly where C) however, their views changed quickly when D) but their views changed quickly when
SAT HACKERS RULE #1	**THE MISUSED "AND"** **The correct answer is D. Use conjunction "and" when the information in the sentence refers to the parallel situation. When two sentences contain opposing views as shown on the above sentences, conjunction 'but' must be used to cancel the previous sentence. Choice C is wrong because 'however' requires a semicolon before however like " ;however,".**

Harder Question 2	Although the new discoveries suggest otherwise, they claim that there are other versions of the Old Testaments.
Middle Question 2	Although the new discoveries suggest otherwise, <u>they</u> claim that there are other versions of the Old Testaments.
Basic Question2	Although the new discoveries suggest otherwise, <u>they</u> claim that there are other versions of the Old Testaments. A) NO CHANGE B) the discoveries C) theologists D) people
SAT HACKERS RULE #2	PRONOUN AND ANTECEDENT NO pronoun can be used independently without an antecedent that indicates pronoun. In this sentence subject "they" either refers to "the new discoveries" or nothing else. Therefore, instead of using "they", the subject must specify "the experts with special knowledge". The correct answer is C.
Harder Question 3	The guest was entertained extravagant by the mayor of the city of North Vancouver, whose city has a strong tie with the guest's company.
Middle Question 3	The guest was entertained <u>extravagant</u> by the mayor of the city of North Vancouver, whose city has a strong tie with the guest's company.
Basic Question3	The guest was entertained <u>extravagant</u> by the mayor of the city of North Vancouver, whose city has a strong tie with the guest's company. A) NO CHANGE B) with extravagance C) extravagantly D) extravagance
SAT HACKERS RULE #3	ADVERBS Adjective cannot modify verb. Simply add "ly" at the end of adjective to make it adverb. The correct answer is C.

Harder Question 4	The New York Times chief editor has decided requiring all articles to be submitted at least one hour before the deadline.
Middle Question 4	The New York Times chief editor has decided <u>requiring</u> all articles to be submitted at least one hour before the deadline.
Basic Question 4	The New York Times chief editor has decided <u>requiring</u> all articles to be submitted at least one hour before the deadline. A) NO CHANGE B) to require C) requesting D) to requiring
SAT HACKERS RULE #4	**PREPOSITIONAL IDIOMS 1 (IDIOMS THAT INDICATE FUTURE ACTION)** **Any verb that indicates "the future action" must use preposition "to", such as "wish to", "hope to", "expect to", "want to", "like to", 'plan to", "suppose to", etc.** **The correct answer is B.**
Harder Question 5	Forty-two years after the Apollo astronauts lands on the moon, new technology has not been developed to initiate the same task easier.
Middle Question 5	Forty-two years after the Apollo astronauts <u>lands</u> on the moon, new technology has not been developed to initiate the same task easier
Basic Question 5	Forty-two years after the Apollo astronauts <u>lands</u> on the moon, new technology has not been developed to initiate the same task easier. A) NO CHANGE B) landed C) had landed D) has landed

| SAT HACKERS RULE #5 | GUESSING THE VERB TENSE BASED ON NON-UNDERLINED SENTENCE |

Be careful with a non-underlined portion on the given sentence because it sometimes indicates what tense should be used. In this question, forty-two years indicates the past. Therefore, the past tense should be used.

Please refer to the following tense chart

PRESENT TENSE	Simple present Present continuous Present perfect	Jason works. Jason is working. Jason has worked.
PAST TENSE	Simple past Past continuous Past perfect	Jason worked. Jason was working. Jason had worked.
FUTURE TENSE	Future Future continuous Future perfect	Jason will work. Jason will be working. Jason will have worked.

More examples

Incorrect: I suspect the Olympic council has a two-tiered vision for the future games: first, it had tried to replace the current exclusive sponsorship; second, it is wanting to add as much capacity to its operation as possible to have more multiple partners.

Correct: I suspect the Olympic council has a two-tiered vision for the future games: first, it tries to replace the current exclusive sponsorship; second, it wants to add as much capacity to its operation as possible to have more multiple partners.

Harder Question 6

Research has revealed that Artificial Intelligence learns a natural algorithm as if human being at a surprisingly fast speed

---

Middle Question 6

Research has revealed that Artificial Intelligence learns a natural algorithm as if human being at a surprisingly fast speed.

Basic Question 6

Research has revealed that Artificial Intelligence learns a natural algorithm as if human being at a surprisingly fast speed.
A) NO CHANGE
B) humankind
C) human being does
D) as fast as human being learns

SAT HACKERS RULE #6	CONDITIONAL 'IF CLAUSE' If clause requires a sentence like choice "C". Choice D is wrong because "as fast as" is already mentioned in the sentence as "a surprisingly fast speed".
Harder Question 7	In a utopian socialism labeled by Henri de Saint-Simon, both rulers and subjects define themselves as the leader of the society.
Middle Question 7	In a utopian socialism labeled by Henri de Saint-Simon, both rulers and subjects define themselves <u>as the leader of the society</u>.
Basic Question 7	In a utopian socialism labeled by Henri de Saint-Simon, both rulers and subjects define themselves <u>as the leader of the society</u>. A) NO CHANGE B) like the leaders of the society C) as the leading people of the society D) as the leaders of the society
SAT HACKERS RULE #7	**SUBJECT NUMBER AGREEMENT** **The preposition "as" indicates the same number of things or people are mentioned. Therefore, 'as the leader' has to be 'as the leaders' (the rulers and subjects).**
Harder Question 8	Meticulous analysis as well as the clinical researches of Parkinson's disease reveal that parts of the symptoms are markedly similar to Down syndrome.
Middle Question 8	Meticulous analysis as well as the clinical researches of Parkinson's disease <u>reveal that the parts of the symptoms are markedly similar to Down syndrome.</u>
Basic Question 8	Meticulous analysis as well as the clinical researches of Parkinson's disease <u>reveal that the parts of the symptoms are markedly similar to Down syndrome.</u> A) reveals that parts of the symptoms are markedly similar to that of Down syndrome B) has been revealing that the parts of the symptoms are markedly similar to Down syndrome. C) has revealed that the parts of the symptoms are markedly similar to Down syndrome. D) reveals that the parts of the symptoms are markedly similar to those of Down

SAT HACKERS RULE #8	SUBJECT-VERB AGREEMENT The subject in this sentence is "analysis", NOT "as well as the clinical researches". Therefore, the verb has to be singular "reveals". Choice C is wrong because "the parts of the symptoms" are being compared to "Down syndrome". The correct answer is D.
Harder Question 9	Of the two pictures, neither the underground main reservoir in the upper valley nor the five auxiliary reservoirs on the ground level are built completely satisfactory.
Middle Question 9	Of the two pictures, neither the underground main reservoir in the upper valley nor the five auxiliary reservoirs <u>on the ground level are built completely satisfactory.</u>
Basic Question 9	Of the two pictures, neither the underground main reservoir in the upper valley nor the five auxiliary reservoirs <u>on the ground level are built completely satisfactory.</u> A) on the ground level are built completely satisfactory. B) on the ground level is built complete satisfaction. C) on the ground level is being built with completely satisfaction. D) on the ground level is built completely satisfactory.
SAT HACKERS RULE #9	**FINDING THE SUBJECT IN "NEITHER ~ NOR"** **The subject in "neither ~ nor" conjunction is what comes after "neither". If the subject after neither is singular, the verb has to be singular.** **In this sentence, "the underground main reservoir" is the subject.** **The correct answer is D. Choice B is wrong because it uses "noun, satisfaction".**
Harder Question 10	Cindy cherished the moment of the day when her and her mother, Caroline met the president of Walmart in recognition of the best employees of the year ceremony.
Middle Question 10	Cindy cherished the moment of the day <u>when her and her mother, Caroline met</u> the president of Walmart in recognition of the best employees of the year ceremony.

Basic Question 10	Cindy cherished the moment of the day <u>when her and her mother, Caroline met</u> the president of Walmart in recognition of the best employees of the year ceremony. A) when she and her mother, Caroline met B) when her and her mother, Caroline had met C) when she and her mother, Caroline have met D) when her and her mother, Caroline will meet
SAT HACKERS RULE #10	**USAGE OF SUBJECTIVE PRONOUN AFTER THE CONJUNCTION** Conjunction "when" requires subject. In this sentence, "she" instead of "her" is the correct form. Choice C is wrong because subordinate clause starting with the conjunction "when" contains the present perfect tense. The correct answer is A.
Harder Question 11	The disgruntled shopper had a tendency of claiming a refund for the goods he fully used, perhaps out of expectation at having to receive courtesy gift cards in the past.
Middle Question 11	The disgruntled shopper had a <u>tendency of claiming</u> a refund for the goods he fully used, perhaps out of expectation at having to receive courtesy gift cards in the past.
Basic Question 11	The disgruntled shopper had a <u>tendency of claiming</u> a refund for the goods he fully used, perhaps out of expectation at having to receive courtesy gift cards in the past. A) tendency to claiming B) tendency to claim C) intention of claiming D) intention to claim
SAT HACKERS RULE #11	**PREPOSITIONAL IDIOM 2** Just as introduced on SAT HACKERS Rule #4, a word, "tendency" has the future concept. therefore, the proper idiomatic preposition "to" must be used. Choice A is wrong because "to+Verb" is the right form, not "to+Verb~ing". Choice D is wrong because it changes the meaning. The correct answer is B.

Harder Question 12	**Korean filmmaker Kim Sun Tak is like the filmmaker Alysia Syndayun in his use of ethnic backgrounds, but unlike his film, she dwells on the religious aspects of her film characters**
Middle Question 12	Korean filmmaker Kim Sun Tak is like the filmmaker Alysia Syndayun in his use of ethnic backgrounds, <u>but unlike his film, she</u> dwells on the religious aspects of her film characters
Basic Question 12	Korean filmmaker Kim Sun Tak is like the filmmaker Alysia Syndayun in his use of ethnic backgrounds, <u>but unlike his film, she</u> dwells on the religious aspects of her film characters A) however unlike him, she B) but unlike him, she C) ;however, unlike his film, she D) but unlike the film he directed, she
SAT HACKERS RULE #12	**USAGE OF "UNLIKE"** **Preposition "unlike" requires exactly the same form of word that it tries to compare. In this sentence, the subject "she" is being compared to his film. Therefore B is the only answer.**
Harder Question 13	Donald Trump has received many complaints about his recent Republican presidential nomination speech, which some audience condemn to be extreme.
Middle Question 13	Donald Trump has received many complaints about his recent Republican presidential nomination speech, which some audience <u>condemn to be extreme</u>.
Basic Question 13	Donald Trump has received many complaints about his recent Republican presidential nomination speech, which some audience <u>condemn to be extreme</u>. A) condemn to have been extreme B) condemn to be extremely C) condemned to be extreme D) condemned to have been extremely

SAT HACKERS RULE #13	PAST FORM OF "TO BE" The main sentence indicates that Donald Trump has already received complaints. It is impossible to use "to be" which indicates the future action. Therefore, the answer is A, which indicates the audience condemn to what had happened in the past.
Harder Question 14	The mutual relationship between the 2016 Brazil Olympic organizer and its sponsors are truly symbiotic, for neither can promote activities without each other.
Middle Question 14	The mutual relationship between the 2016 Brazil Olympic organizer and its sponsors <u>are truly symbiotic</u>, for neither can promote activities without each other.
Basic Question 14	The mutual relationship between the 2016 Brazil Olympic organizer and its sponsors <u>are truly symbiotic</u>, for neither can promote activities without each other. A) is truly symbiotic B) is in true symbiotic relation C) are in true symbiotic relations D) are nothing but truly symbiotic
SAT HACKERS RULE #14	**FINDING SUBJECT** **The "relationship" in this sentence is the only subject, which is singular. Therefore, A is the correct answer. Any word(s) that comes after the preposition is not a subject. In this sentence, "between the 2015 Brazil Olympic organizer and its sponsors" is the prepositional phrase.**
Harder Question 15	As the challenger throbbed in, the UFC heavyweight champion cringed, the challenger's blowing-out-punch more strong, and winding up the champ's last-ditch effort.
Middle Question 15	As the challenger throbbed in, the UFC heavyweight champion cringed, <u>the challenger's</u> <u>blowing-out-punch more strong,</u> and winding up the champ's last-ditch effort.

Ch. 1   Ch. 2   Ch. 3   Ch. 4   Ch. 5   Ch. 6   Ch. 7   Ch. 8   Ch. 9   **Ch. 10**

Basic Question 15	As the challenger throbbed in, the UFC heavyweight champion cringed, <u>the challenger's blowing-out-punch more strong,</u> and winding up the champ's last-ditch effort. A) the challenger's blowing-out-punch more stronger B) the challenger's blowing-out-punch more strongly C) the challenger blew out punch more stronger D) ; the challenger blew out punch more stronger
SAT HACKERS RULE #15	COMPARISON (MORE vs. ~er) With a one-syllable word or a word ending in -y or –ly, add the suffix -er to form a comparative phrase. With an adjective or adverb of more-than-one syllable, use more to create the comparative phrase. In this sentence, all the choice contains comparative "more". Therefore, the only option available to us is to convert adjective "strong" to adverb. "strongly". Choice B is the answer.
Harder Question 16	Clearly, the products will have been less appealing if the head designer had not tried to disperse the design concept in Youtube.
Middle Question 16	Clearly, <u>the products will have been less appealing</u> if the head designer had not tried to disperse the design concept in Youtube
Basic Question 16	Clearly, <u>the products will have been less appealing</u> if the head designer had not tried to disperse the design concept in Youtube. A) the products will be less appealing B) the products would be been less appealing C) the products would have been less appealing D) the products might be less appealing

SAT HACKERS RULE #16	PAST PERFECT CONDITIONAL IF CLAUSE The correct answer C.	
	If clause (conditional clause)	**Main clause (consequence)**
	If + past perfect (had + p.p)	perfect conditional (would have/could have/should have/must have/might have/may have)
	If Jason had seen the accident,	He would have been fainted

Harder Question 17	The amiable relation between Jason and I ended as soon as we each moved out on our own.

Middle Question 17	The amiable relation <u>between Jason and I ended</u> as soon as we each moved out on our own.

Basic Question 17	The amiable relation <u>between Jason and I ended</u> as soon as we each moved out on our own. A) between Jason and me ended B) between Jason and myself ended C) between Jason and I end D) between Jason and me would end

SAT HACKERS RULE #17	USAGE OF PRONOUN AFTER PREPOSITION The pronoun after the preposition must be objective. NOT SUBJECTIVE. In this sentence, the preposition "between" contains subjective pronoun "I", which should be changed to an objective form "me" the correct answer is A. Choice D is wrong in that it uses "would", a model verb that has a meaning of repetition in the past.

Harder Question 18	Being cancelled the job interview appointment that the company mailed to participate, Jason never cancelled another job interview again.

Middle Question 18	<u>Being cancelled</u> the job interview appointment that the company mailed to participate, Jason never cancelled another job interview again.

Basic Question 18	<u>Being cancelled</u> the job interview appointment that the company mailed to participate, Jason never cancelled another job interview again. A) Cancelled B) Cancelling C) Having cancelled D) After he made a cancellation on
SAT HACKERS RULE #18	USAGE OF HAVING + P.P. ~ PAST TENSE The verb in the main sentence is past tense, and the subordinate clause indicates that the cancellation had occurred before, showing the clear time shifting. In that case, HAVING +P.P. phrase should be applied. Having cancelled (After Jason had cancelled~). Therefore, the correct answer is C. D is wrong in that the sentence used unnecessary "made" as a verb.
Harder Question 19	In a world that the government has less and less control to terrorism, cold comfort has become a normal trend now.
Middle Question 19	<u>In a world that the government has less and less control</u> to terrorism, cold comfort has become a normal trend now.
Basic Question 19	<u>In a world that the government has less and less control</u> to terrorism, cold comfort has become a normal trend now. A) In a world in which the government has less control B) In a world where the government has less and less control C) In a world that the government has no control D) In a world that the government has significantly reducing control
SAT HACKERS RULE #19	WHERE vs. THAT Don't be confused between the conjunctions "where" and "that". "that" should not be used as a conjunction for a place. Therefore, B should be the answer. Choice A is wrong as it changed its original meaning.

Harder Question 20	Because airplane travels allow people to reach around the world drastically faster and more convenient, some have claimed the concept of borderline is radically different than earlier times.
Middle Question 20	Because airplane travels allow people to reach around the world drastically faster and more convenient, some have claimed the concept of borderline <u>is radically different than earlier times</u>.
Basic Question 20	Because airplane travels allow people to reach around the world drastically faster and more convenient, some have claimed the concept of borderline <u>is radically different than earlier times.</u> A) has become radically different than earlier times B) is radically different than that of earlier times C) is drastically and radically different than that of earlier times D) is drastically different than that in earlier times
SAT HACKERS RULE #20	FAULTY COMPARISON: COMPARE APPLE TO APPLE In this sentence, the concept of borderline is being compared with earlier times. Therefore, Choice B should be the correct answer. Choice C is wrong because of redundant error (drastically and radically). Choice D is wrong because preposition "in" instead of "of" is used. More examples Incorrect: Some experts I spoke with said that a self-driving car population is closer at hand than one populated with trucks. Correct: Some experts I spoke with said that a future populated with self-driving cars is closer at hand than one populated with trucks. Incorrect: Sometimes, the mysteries about Elvis Presly is more cryptic than Shakespeare. Correct: Sometimes, the mysteries about Elvis Presly is more cryptic than <u>those about</u> Shakespeare.

Harder Question 21	Ford's first vehicle Model A, which was first owned by Ernest Pfennig, a Chicago dentist, and capable of a top speed of five miles per hour.
Middle Question 21	Ford's first vehicle Model A, which was first owned by Ernest Pfennig, <u>a Chicago dentist, and capable of a top speed of five miles per hour.</u>
Basic Question 21	Ford's first vehicle Model A, which was first owned by Ernest Pfennig, <u>a Chicago dentist, and capable of a top speed of five miles per hour.</u> A) a Chicago dentist, and capability of a top speed B) a Chicago dentist, and capable to a top speed C) a Chicago dentist, was capable of a top speed D) a Chicago dentist was able to provide a capacity of a top speed
SAT HACKERS RULE #21	MISSING VERB The sentence does not contain a main verb. Therefore, C should be the only answer. Choice D is wordy.
Harder Question 22	When Clarence Anglin escaped the Alcatraz prison on a handcrafted rubber boat in June 11, 1962, with two other inmates, John Anglin and Frank Morris, he had realized that he had left a note for a destination under his mattress.
Middle Question 22	When Clarence Anglin escaped the Alcatraz prison on a handcrafted rubber boat in June 11, 1962, with two other inmates, John Anglin and Frank Morris, <u>he had realized that he had left</u> a note for a destination under his mattress.
Basic Question 22	When Clarence Anglin escaped the Alcatraz prison on a handcrafted rubber boat in June 11, 1962, with two other inmates, John Anglin and Frank Morris, <u>he had realized that he had left</u> a note for a destination under his mattress. A) NO CHANGE B) Clarence had realized that Frank had left C) he realized that Frank had left D) Clarence had realized that Frank left

SAT HACKERS RULE #22	**DISTINGUISHING PRONOUN** When two or three identical-gender people are in one sentence, it is necessary to identify who is referring the second person. In this sentence, choice C is correct because "he" in the main clause obviously indicates Clarence. Choice B and D is wrong because of tense error.
Harder Question 23	That women and black people have to be given the enfranchisement were considered a radical idea in eighteenth-century America.
Middle Question 23	That women and black people <u>have to be given the enfranchisement were considered</u> a radical idea in eighteenth-century America.
Basic Question 23	That women and black people <u>have to be given the enfranchisement were considered</u> a radical idea in eighteenth-century America. A) have to be given the enfranchisement were considered B) has to be given the enfranchisement were considered C) have to be given the enfranchisement was considered D) has to be given the enfranchisement was considered
SAT HACKERS RULE #23	**A PACKAGE INFORMATION USING <u>SUBORDINATE THAT CLAUSES</u>** A package information using subordinate conjunction "that" should be considered as a singular subject. Therefore, choice C should be the correct answer.
Harder Question 24	The concerned parents were anxious to see that their teenage children had drove the parents' vehicles recklessly.
Middle Question 24	The concerned parents were anxious to see that their teenage children <u>had drove</u> the parents' vehicles recklessly.
Basic Question 24	The concerned parents were anxious to see that their teenage children <u>had drove</u> the parents' vehicles recklessly. A) had droven B) had driven C) have drove D) drive

SAT HACKERS RULE #24	**IRREGULAR VERB FORM** Drive -> drove -> driven. Therefore, the correct answer is B *appendix A for the irregular verb lists
Harder Question 25	Though the board members' criteria to select a new CEO for the company were both judicious as well as meticulous, the majority stockholders followed their own preference, thereby stifling the upcoming election.
Middle Question 25	Though the board members' criteria to select a new CEO for the company <u>were both judicious as well as meticulous,</u> the majority stockholders followed their own preference, thereby stifling the upcoming election.
Basic Question 25	Though the board members' criteria to select a new CEO for the company <u>were both judicious as well as meticulous,</u> the majority stockholders followed their own preference, thereby stifling the upcoming election. A) was both judicious as well as meticulous B) was both judicious and meticulous C) were both judicious as well as meticulous D) were both judicious and meticulous
SAT HACKERS RULE #25	**BOTH ~ AND + PLURAL SUBJECT** Idiom cannot be replaced with other form of preposition. Criteria is plural, while criterion is singular. Therefore, the correct answer is B.
Harder Question 26	Concerned that recruiting new students was challenging last year, the university announced several scholarship plans in order for increasing international students.
Middle Question 26	Concerned that recruiting students was challenging last year, the university announced several scholarship plans in order <u>for increasing international students.</u>

Basic Question 26	Concerned that recruiting students was challenging last year, the university announced several scholarship plans in order <u>for increasing international students</u>. A) to increasing international students. B) to increase international students. C) for increment of international students. D) to make increase international students.
SAT HACKERS RULE #26	SIMPLIFICATION When you have two choices left out, always pick the choice with a simple version. In this sentence, choice D "make increase" can be reduced to "increase". Therefore, the answer should be B.
Harder Question 27	Although the professor's promise " a complete open book test" suggested the final would be easy, students found it not that simple as they had expected.
Middle Question 27	Although the professor's promise " a complete open book test" suggested the final would be easy, <u>students found it not that simple</u> as they had expected.
Basic Question 27	Although the professor's promise " a complete open book test" suggested the final would be easy, <u>students found it not that simple</u> as they had expected. A) students find it not that simple B) students found them not that simple C) students found it not as simple D) students did not find it that simple
SAT HACKERS RULE #27	AS ~ AS The correct answer is C. Conjunction "That" cannot be replaced to adverb "as"
Harder Question 28	The staff favored the new stock option plan, a scheme in which the company's local divisions, rather than the reluctant head office, decides how best to allocate profit equally.

Middle Question 28	The staff favored the new stock option plan, <u>a scheme in which the company's local divisions, rather than the reluctant head office, decides how best to allocate</u> profit equally.
Basic Question 28	The staff favored the new stock option plan, <u>a scheme in which the company's local divisions, rather than the reluctant head office, decides how best to allocate</u> profit equally. A) a scheme was that the company's local divisions, rather than the reluctant head office, decides how best to allocate B) a scheme is that the company's local divisions, rather than the reluctant head office, decides how best to allocate C) a scheme in which the company's local divisions, rather than the reluctant head office, decides how best to allocate D) a scheme in which the company's local divisions, rather than the reluctant head office, decide how best to allocate
SAT HACKERS RULE #28	COMMA SPLICE Choice A and B are comma splice error in that both sentences try to combine two sentences using comma. The original sentence violates the subject and verb agreement as the subject, "divisions" is plural, which requires plural verb form, "decide". Therefore, the correct answer is D
Harder Question 29	Results of the gloomy economic forecast in the upcoming fourth quarter sales, the CEO decides to sacrifice his perk, salary increase, and his merger plan.
Middle Question 29	<u>Results of</u> the gloomy economic forecast in the upcoming fourth quarter sales, the CEO decided to sacrifice his perk, salary increase, and his merger plan.
Basic Question 29	<u>Results of</u> the gloomy economic forecast in the upcoming fourth quarter sales, the CEO decided to sacrifice his perk, salary increase, and his merger plan. A) NO CHANGE B) Results by C) Resulted by D) Resulting in

SAT HACKERS RULE #29	**TENSE ON ADVERBIAL PHRASE** The main sentence uses the past tense "decided". Therefore, Choice C "resulted by" must be the answer.
Harder Question 30	Without unanimity or no muted return, the UN security council in the meeting is entirely dependent upon the chairperson's final decision to send the UN peace corps to the conflicted region in Syria.
Middle Question 30	<u>Without unanimity or no muted return,</u> the UN security council in the meeting is entirely dependent upon the chairperson's final decision to send the UN peace corps to the conflicted region in Syria.
Basic Question 30	<u>Without unanimity or no muted return,</u> the UN security council in the meeting is entirely dependent upon the chairperson's final decision to send the UN peace corps to the conflicted region in Syria. A) Without unanimity or any muted return, B) Neither unanimity or no muted return, C) Neither unanimity or muted return, D) Either unanimity or no muted return,
SAT HACKERS RULE #30	**DOUBLE NEGATIVE** Preposition "without" is already negative. Having another negative word "No" makes double negative error. Therefore, the correct answer is A.
Harder Question 31	Working with new people, or even re-organizing the old employees to a new branch, are always a daunting task, especially when there is little consensus about the products it carries.
Middle Question 31	Working with new people, or even re-organizing the old employees to a new branch, <u>are always a daunting task,</u> especially when there is little consensus about the products it carries.

Ch. 1 Ch. 2 Ch. 3 Ch. 4 Ch. 5 Ch. 6 Ch. 7 Ch. 8 Ch. 9 **Ch. 10**

Basic Question 31	Working with new people, or even re-organizing the old employees to a new branch, <u>are</u> always a daunting task, especially when there is little consensus about the products it carries. A) are always a daunting task B) is always a daunting task C) always are a daunting task D) has always a daunting task
SAT HACKERS RULE #31	USING GERUND PHRASE AS A SUBJECT Gerund phrase is treated as a singular subject. Therefore, the correct answer is B.
Harder Question 32	Those buyers who bought houses just before the subprime mortgage crisis in 2008 were either lucky or exceptional astute.
Middle Question 32	Those buyers who bought houses just before the subprime mortgage crisis in 2008 <u>were</u> <u>either lucky</u> or exceptional astute.
Basic Question 32	Those buyers who bought houses just before the subprime mortgage crisis in 2008 <u>were either lucky or exceptional astute.</u> A) were either lucky or exceptional astute B) were neither lucky nor exceptional astute C) were either lucky or exceptionally astute D) were neither lucky nor exceptionally astute
SAT HACKERS RULE #32	FINDING AN OPPOSING MEANING The sentence must be negative in its tone. Therefore, choice D, which follows negative form and uses the correct neither ~ nor idiom is the answer.
Harder Question 33	Some of the glacial sediment deposits support the evidence that the Ice Age effected every continent except South America.
Middle Question 33	Some of the glacial sediment deposits support the evidence that the Ice Age <u>effected</u> every continent except South America.
Basic Question 33	Some of the glacial sediment deposits support the evidence that the Ice Age <u>effected</u> every continent except South America. A) effected B) was affected C) affected D) inflicted
SAT HACKERS RULE #33	CONFUSING WORD: AFFECT VS. EFFECT Affect is commonly used as a verb, while effect is used for noun. Therefore, the correct form, "affected" should be used. *Appendix C for the confusing word list

Harder Question 34	The radiation emitted by high-intensity-discharge microwave oven is very effective in activating molecules foods inside the oven much like the way of electromagnetic waves that zap through the air from TV or radio transmitters, thereby it allows to cook or boil foods safer and faster.
Middle Question 34	The radiation emitted by high-intensity-discharge microwave oven is very effective in activating molecules <u>foods inside the oven much like the way of electromagnetic waves</u> that zap through the air from TV or radio transmitters, thereby it allows to cook or boil foods safer and faster.
Basic Question 34	The radiation emitted by high-intensity-discharge microwave oven is very effective in activating molecules <u>foods inside the oven much like the way of electromagnetic waves</u> that zap through the air from TV or radio transmitters, thereby it allows to cook or boil foods safer and faster. A) ; foods inside the oven, much like the way of electromagnetic waves that zap through the air from TV or radio transmitters, thereby it allows to cook or boil foods safer and faster. B) ; foods inside the oven much like the way of electromagnetic waves zap through the air from TV or radio transmitters, thereby it allows to cook or boil foods safer and faster. C) : foods inside the oven much like the way of electromagnetic waves that zap through the air from TV or radio transmitters, cook or boil foods safer and faster. D) : foods inside the oven, much like the way of electromagnetic waves that zap through the air from TV or radio transmitters, are cooked or boiled safer and faster.
SAT HACKERS RULE #34	RUN-ON SENTENCE (a sentence that contains multiple independent clauses without having a proper conjunction) The original sentence contains run-on sentence, showing no clear indication which is subject and verb. Choices B,C have no verb.

Harder Question 35	The Vancouver aquarium is submitted business proposals to several municipal governments in Alberta in the hope to get funds to establish an exotic tropical tube.
Middle Question 35	The Vancouver aquarium <u>is submitted business proposals to several municipal governments in Alberta in the hope to get</u> funds to establish an exotic tropical tube.
Basic Question 35	The Vancouver <u>aquarium is submitted business proposals to several municipal governments in Alberta in the hope to get</u> funds to establish an exotic tropical tube. A) is submitting business proposals to several municipal governments in Alberta in the hope to get with the hope to get B) is submitting business proposals to several municipal governments in Alberta in the hope of getting C) is being on the process of submission for the business proposals to several municipal governments in Alberta in the hope to get D) is submitting business proposals to several municipal governments in Alberta in the hope to get
SAT HACKERS RULE #35	PREPOSITIONAL PHRASE "IN" The correct form of idiom in this sentence is "in the hope of getting" therefore, the correct answer is B. Prepositional phrase using "in" requires on-going concept. ~ ing.
Harder Question 36	The initial estimation of safely disposing of the toxic wastes is roughly ten times what the Du Pont spent to purchase it in its factory
Middle Question 36	The initial estimation of safely disposing of the toxic wastes is roughly ten times what the Du Pont spent <u>to purchase it</u> in its factory
Basic Question 36	The initial estimation of safely disposing of the toxic wastes is roughly ten times what the Du Pont spent <u>to purchase it</u> in its factory A) for purchasing it B) for the purchase of it C) to purchase its own system D) to purchase them

SAT HACKERS RULE #36	**PRONOUN WITHOUT ANTECEDENT** Pronoun "It" or "them" cannot be used without preceding antecedent in the sentence. Therefore, the correct answer is C.
Harder Question 37	Michael Jorden, Shaquille O'Neal, and Charles Burkley—each of these basketball players was awarded MVP more than once at the time they were playing.
Middle Question 37	Michael Jorden, Shaquille O'Neal, and Charles Burkley—<u>each of these basketball players was awarded MVP more than once at the time they were playing.</u>
Basic Question 37	Michael Jorden, Shaquille O'Neal, and Charles Burkley—each of <u>these basketball players was awarded MVP more than once at the time they were playing.</u> A) NO CHANGE B) each of those basketball players was awarded MVP more than once at the time they were playing C) each of these basketball players were awarded MVP more than once at the time they are playing D) each of these basketball players was awarded MVP more than once at the time he was playing
SAT HACKERS RULE #37	**THE USAGE OF PRONOUN AFTER "EACH" OR "EVERY"** Each or every is always singular form. Therefore, using them is incorrect. The correct answer is D.
Harder Question 38	The theory of quantum mechanics that applies quantum correction compliments classic physics.
Middle Question 38	The theory of quantum mechanics that applies quantum correction <u>compliments classic physics.</u>

Basic Question 38	The theory of quantum mechanics that applies quantum correction <u>compliments classic</u> physics. A) compliments classic physics B) compliment that of classic physics C) complements classic physics D) complement the theory of classic physics
SAT HACKERS RULE #38	CONFUSING WORD: COMPLEMENT VS. COMPLIMENT Complement = fill the gap Compliment = praise The correct answer is D. Appendix C: Confusing words list
Harder Question 39	Some of the hypotheses that Charles Darwin established to explain the origin of species were later rejected as inconsistent to convergent and divergent evolution theories.
Middle Question 39	Some of the hypotheses that Charles Darwin established to explain the origin of species <u>were later rejected as inconsistent to</u> convergent and divergent evolution theories.
Basic Question 39	Some of the hypotheses that Charles Darwin established to explain the origin of species <u>were later rejected as inconsistent to</u> convergent and divergent evolution theories. A) was lately rejected as inconsistent to B) were later rejected like inconsistent to C) were later rejected as inconsistent with D) were later rejected based on inconsistency
SAT HACKERS RULE #39	CONFUSING WORD: LATE vs. LATER. "some" requires plural verb. The correct idiom form in this sentence is "inconsistent with". Therefore, the correct answer is C. Appendix C: Confusing words list

Harder Question 40	<u>For we VIP customers,</u> receiving extensive client care services was eagerly anticipated courtesy programs at the mall.
Middle Question 40	<u>For we VIP customers,</u> receiving extensive client care services was eagerly anticipated courtesy programs at the mall.
Basic Question 40	<u>For we VIP customers,</u> receiving extensive client care services was eagerly anticipated courtesy programs at the mall. A) For we, VIP customers, B) For us, VIP customers, C) For we and VIP customers, D) For us as VIP customers,
SAT HACKERS RULE #40	PRONOUN AFTER A PREPOSITION Always use object pronoun after preposition The correct answer is B. choice D is wrong because "as" is not needed.
Harder Question 41	Fully automated vehicles are a work in progress, an autonomous vehicle that drives without any human interaction, parks parallel along a narrow girder, and sending an emergency signal to the driver when it is required.
Middle Question 41	Fully automated vehicles are a work in progress, an autonomous vehicle that drives without any human interaction, parks parallel along a narrow girder, <u>and sending an emergency signal to the driver</u> when it is required.
Basic Question 41	Fully automated vehicles are a work in progress, an autonomous vehicle that drives without any human interaction, parks parallel along a narrow girder, <u>and sending an emergency signal to the driver</u> when it is required. A) as well as sends an emergency signal to the driver B) and was capable of sending an emergency signal to the driver C) and also sends an emergency signal by the driver D) and sends an emergency signal to the driver
SAT HACKERS RULE #41	PARALLELISM "drives, parks, and sends" is the correct form of parallelism. Choice C is wrong because "also" is not needed. The correct answer is D.

Harder Question 42	On the final exam, three exactly same identical questions appeared that have been miscalculated on the midterm test.
Middle Question 42	On the final exam, <u>three exactly same identical questions appeared that have been</u> miscalculated on the midterm test.
Basic Question 42	On the final exam, <u>three exactly same identical questions appeared that have been</u> <u>miscalculated</u> on the midterm test. A) three exactly same identical questions appeared that were miscalculated B) three identical questions appeared that have been miscalculated C) three identical questions had appeared that have been miscalculated D) three identical questions appeared that had been miscalculated
SAT HACKERS RULE #42	REDUNDANT / GUESSING THE TENSE Three exactly same = identical The midterm test should have taken before the final, and must be the past perfect. Therefore, the correct answer is D. As shown on the above question, overused unnecessary words should be simply deleted, although it may sound more academic and specific. More examples Roughly about the year of 2030's, we will see more drones in the air than cars on the roads.
Harder Question 43	Novelist Georgy Orwell's accounts of all animals are equal, but some animals are more equal than others begin with the author's allegory of the Russian Revolution and culminated with his reminiscence of his past
Middle Question 43	Novelist Georgy Orwell's accounts of all animals are equal, but some animals are more equal than <u>others begin with the author's allegory of the Russian Revolution and culminated</u> with his reminiscence of his past

Basic Question 43	Novelist Georgy Orwell's accounts of all animals are equal, but some animals are more equal than others <u>begin with the author's allegory of the Russian Revolution and</u> <u>culminated with</u> his reminiscence of his past A) begin with the author's allegory of the Russian Revolution and culminate with B) has began with the author's allegory of the Russian Revolution and has culminated with C) began with the author's allegory of the Russian Revolution and culminate with D) begins with the author's allegory of the Russian Revolution and culminates with
SAT HACKERS RULE #43	USING THE SAME VERB TENSE IN PARALLEL STRUCTURE Descriptive sentence such as a natural phenomenon or announcement use the simple present tense. Therefore, the correct answer is A. Choice D violates the subject-verb agreement. (subject = accounts)
Harder Question 44	The maid at the hotel asked "does the room temperature right for yourself and your family?"
Middle Question 44	The maid at the hotel asked "does the room temperature right <u>for yourself and your</u> <u>family?"</u>
Basic Question 44	The maid at the hotel asked "is the room temperature right <u>for yourself and your</u> <u>family?"</u> A) for yours and your family?" B) for you and your family?" C) for yourselves ?" D) for your and your family?"
SAT HACKERS RULE #44	REFLECTIVE PRONOUN "~SELF" Reflective pronoun cannot be used alone. Therefore, the correct answer is B. the funny thing is that after the "Brexit", British people speak each other this way, showing an exaggerated courtesy inflicted by economic concern.

 Ch. 1

 Ch. 2

 Ch. 3

 Ch. 4

 Ch. 5

 Ch. 6

 Ch. 7

 Ch. 8

 Ch. 9

Ch. 10

Harder Question 45	Every summer my parents invite their relatives, those people come for a family reunion.
Middle Question 45	Every summer my parents invite their relatives, <u>those people</u> come for a family reunion.
Basic Question 45	Every summer my parents invite their relatives, <u>those people</u> come for a family reunion. A) who come B) the people come C) their people come D) who are invited over in order to
SAT HACKERS RULE #45	CONJUNCTION WHO Use "who" for people The correct answer is A. Choice D is wordy.
Harder Question 46	Down the road from the school, my brother attend, Seven Twelve convenient store is always open, and some customers are always there.
Middle Question 46	Down the road from the <u>school, my brother attend</u>, Seven Twelve convenient store is always open, and some customers are always there.
Basic Question 46	Down the road from the <u>school, my brother attend</u>, Seven Twelve convenient store is always open, and some customers are always there. A) school, my brother attends, B) school, my brother attends C) school my brother attends D) school, which is my brother attends,
SAT HACKERS RULE #46	OMITTING "THAT" Conjunction "that" can be omitted and having comma is not necessary in the place of "that". Therefore, the correct answer is C

Harder Question 47	It is comforting to see that the Seven Twelve store. And its customers are always there.
Middle Question 47	It is comforting to see that the <u>Seven Twelve store. And its customers</u> are always there.
Basic Question 47	It is comforting to see that the <u>Seven Twelve store. And its customers</u> are always there. A) NO CHANGE B) Seven Twelve store and that its customers C) Seven Twelve store and its customers D) Seven Twelve store and with its customers
SAT HACKERS RULE #47	USAGE OF VERB "that" is conjunction, which requires a verb. Therefore, the correct answer is C.
Harder Question 48	The police's reasoning implied that, even if the robber was wearing a mask, it had enough knowledge to collect the evidences such as the robber's height matching the suspect, weight, and foot size.
Middle Question 48	The police's reasoning implied that, <u>even if the robber was wearing a mask, it had enough knowledge to collect the evidences such as the robber's height matching the suspect, weight, and foot size.</u>

Ch. 1
Ch. 2
Ch. 3
Ch. 4
Ch. 5
Ch. 6
Ch. 7
Ch. 8
Ch. 9
Ch. 10

Basic Question 48	The police's reasoning implied that, <u>even if the robber was wearing a mask, it had enough knowledge to collect the evidences such as the robber's height matching the suspect, weight, and foot size.</u>
	A) even if the robber was wearing a mask the officer had enough knowledge to collect the evidences such as: the height, weight, and foot size.
	B) ,even if the robber was wearing a mask, the officer had enough knowledge to collect the evidences: the robber's height matching the suspect, weight, and foot size.
	C) ,even if the robber was wearing a mask, the officer had enough knowledge to collect the evidences; the height, weight, and foot size.
	D) ,even if the robber was wearing a mask, the officer had enough knowledge to collect the evidences: the height, weight, and foot size.
SAT HACKERS RULE #48	COLON
	In SAT, the Collegeboard asks the single most important purpose of colon: to introduce things.
	It can introduce just about anything: a list of words, a list of phrases, a list of clauses.
	Ex)
	Monkey has only one desire on its mind: banana.
	Monkey has only one desire on its mind: a pile of banana.
	Monkey has only one desire on its mind: it wants to have a pile of banana.
	Monkey has three desires on its mind: finding banana trees, piling banana, eating banana.
	Now compare the following two sentences
	Apple corporation's cellphone beats its competitors specifically in the core area of waterproof functionality.
	Apple corporation's cellphone beats its competitors specifically in the core area: waterproof functionality.
	As seen on the above comparisons, the main function of colon is not only to introduce things, but also emphasizes what the writer wishes to emphasize.
	If you are not sure whether to use colon or not, just imagine a word "that is". In other word, "that is" is used the same as colon.

SAT HACKERS RULE #48	COLON (continued)
	-Monkey has only one desire on its mind\<that is\>banana.
	-Monkey has only one desire on its mind\<that is\>a pile of banana.
	-Monkey has only one desire on its mind\<that is\>it wants to have a pile of banana.
	-Monkey has three desires on its mind\<that is:\>finding banana trees, piling banana, eating banana.
	Colon, however, cannot be used in the middle of incomplete sentence that obstructs the flow of the sentence.
	Correct: Apple specializes in high-tech gadgets: cellphone, ipad, and computer.
	Incorrect: Apple specializes in : high-tech gadgets such as cellphone, ipad, and computer.
	Choice A is wrong for two reasons: first, it misses comma; Second, such as before the colon is not only unnecessary, but also makes the previous sentence incomplete.
	Choice B is wrong because the phrase "robber's height matching the suspect" does not parallel with the following words, "weigh, and foot size"
	Choice C is wrong because of the misusage of semi-colon in the place of colon.
Harder Question 49	**However they choose their dormitory, college students at St. Johns are not entirely allowed to make their own decisions in choosing their roommates; as a result, many students choose off-campus apartment.**
Middle Question 49	However <u>they choose their dormitory, college students at St. Johns are not entirely allowed</u> to make their own decisions in <u>choosing their roommates; as a result,</u> many students choose off-campus apartment.

Basic Question 49	However <u>they choose their dormitory, college students at St. Johns are not entirely allowed to make their own decisions in choosing their roommates; as a result,</u> many students choose off-campus apartment. A) they choose their dormitory, college students at St. Johns are not entirely allowed to make their own decisions in choosing their roommates as a result, B) they choose their dormitory, college students at St. Johns are not entirely allowed to make their own decisions in choosing their roommates, as a result, C) they choose their dormitory, college students at St. Johns are not entirely allowed to make their own decisions in choosing their roommates; as a result, D) college students choose their dormitory, college students at St. Johns are not entirely allowed to make their own decisions to choose their roommates; and as a result,
SAT HACKERS RULE #49	**SEMICOLON** The semicolon is used between two independent clauses. Semicolon functions as a conjunction. Therefore, semi-colon cannot be used along with a coordinating conjunction (*for, and, nor, but, or, yet, so*). Ex) Only the authorized apple service centre can replace the original apple parts; unauthorized service center can provide a repair service using generic parts. Only the authorized apple service centre can replace the original apple parts, but unauthorized service center can provide a repair service using generic parts. As seen on the above examples, the semi-colon can be used when two opposite opinions are presented in both sentences. Ex) The number of drunken drivers continues to fall; consequently, the police focuses more on parking violations or speeding. Ex) Some physicians' handwriting makes it extremely difficult to read; accordingly, all doctors' prescriptions for drugs are required to be recorded in the internet website that links between medical doctors and pharmacies in the country. As seen on the above examples, the semi-colon can be used in place of transitional expressions such as *accordingly, consequently, for example, nevertheless, so, thus*. "However" in this sentence is used as a adverb meaning "to whatever extent or degree". The conjunctive adverb, "as a result," is requires the semi-colon. Therefore, the correct answer is C.

Harder Question 50	As New York Times reported last year, Honda's airbag scandals have gone so far as to set up something of the comprehensive double-dealing—an intentional inspection report forgery and fraud from the board members—to inflate the sales, while avoiding critical industry standards test.
Middle Question 50	As New York Times reported last year, Honda's airbag scandals have gone so far as to set up something of the comprehensive <u>double-dealing—an intentional inspection report forgery and fraud from the board members—to inflate the sales, while avoiding critical industry standards test.</u>
Basic Question 50	As New York Times reported last year, Honda's airbag scandals have gone so far as to set up something of the comprehensive <u>double-dealing—an intentional inspection report forgery and fraud from the board members—to inflate the sales, while avoiding critical industry standards test.</u> A) double-dealing—an intentional inspection report forgery and fraud from the board members—to inflate the sales, while avoiding critical industry standards test. B) double-dealing, an intentional inspection report forgery and fraud from the board members to inflate the sales, while avoiding critical industry standards test. C) double-dealing with an intentional inspection report forgery and fraud from the board members—to inflate the sales, while avoiding critical industry standards test. D) double-dealing and an intentional inspection report forgery and fraud from the board members—to inflate the sales, while avoiding critical industry standards test.

Ch. 1 Ch. 2 Ch. 3 Ch. 4 Ch. 5 Ch. 6 Ch. 7 Ch. 8 Ch. 9 **Ch. 10**

SAT HACKERS RULE #50	DASHES Dash or dashes function as super-comma, serving some of the same functions as commas and colons) Dashes are used to set off interrupting clauses or phrases to call more attention to what lies in between: -Daniel pleaded guilty; the only allegation presented by the police for the jury was whether the evidence was collected legally or —as the judge, Mr.Ryan argued—was premeditated and fabricated. Choice B is wrong because comma is missing after the word, "members" Choice C is wrong because "to infinitive clause" (to inflate the sales, while avoiding critical industry standards test.) is not connected directly to the main sentence that originally meant to modify. Choice D is wrong because of using conjunction 'and' in place of dash.
Harder Question 51	The secretary of internal affairs picked the house speaker Paul Ryan as a next candidate for the position—a dynamic colleague in Washington.
Middle Question 51	The secretary of internal affairs picked the house speaker Paul Ryan as a next candidate for the position—a dynamic colleague in Washington.
Basic Question 51	The secretary of internal affairs picked the house speaker Paul Ryan as a next candidate for the position—a dynamic colleague in Washington. A) position—a dynamic colleague in Washington. B) position; a dynamic colleague in Washington. C) position, who is a dynamic colleague in Washington. D) position with a dynamic colleague in Washington.

SAT HACKERS RULE #51	DASH One dash functions just as the way the colon does. Therefore, they are interchangeable. The police who saw the shooting felt that the robber had more time to run away than confront the police—the more time the police felt the robber had, the more likely the robber were in his intention to kill the shopkeeper. Choice B is wrong because semicolon cannot be linked with a phrase Choice C is wrong because of the misplaced modifier error. "who" is linked with the position. Therefore, who makes ambiguous whether it refers to the secretary of internal affairs or the house speaker Paul Ryan. Choice D is wrong for the same reason as C.
Harder Question 52	That nickel and dime store where I used to buy stationery, when I was only five year old kid, was abandoned, leaving only a faded signage on the roof of the building.
Middle Question 52	<u>That nickel and dime store where I used to buy stationery, when I was only five year old kid,</u> was abandoned, leaving only a faded signage on the roof of the building.
Basic Question 52	<u>That nickel and dime store where I used to buy stationery ,when I was only five year old kid,</u> was abandoned, leaving only a faded signage on the roof of the building. A) That nickel-and-dime store where I used to buy stationery ,when I was only a five-year-old kid, B) That nickel and dime store where I used to buy stationery ,when I was only a five year old kid, C) When I was only a five year old kid, I used to buy stationary at that nickel-and-dime store D) I used to buy stationery at that nickel-and-dime store when I was only five year old kid

SAT HACKERS RULE #52	HYPHEN
	Hyphen is mainly used as an adjective by joining two or more words together. Example sentences using the hyphen as a compound adjectives -The employer is fed up with his do-nothing secretary. -That thirteen-year-old girl got pregnant is not a big news in some parts of Africa. -We cannot give you with a money-back guarantee under this discount term. -The newly introduced iphone is not quite a state-of-the-art technology. Choice B is wrong because "nickel-and-dime" is the correct form to be used as an adjective for store. Choice C is wrong because "a five-year-old" is the correct form to be used as an adjective for kid. C also makes the comma splice error. Choice D is wrong because it changes the original meaning by misplacing the modifier to make it sound like the kid was abandoned.
Harder Question 53	The present interreligious conflicts in France, which was ignited by the extreme Jihadist, turned the entire Europe in turmoil.
Middle Question 53	The present interreligious conflicts in <u>France, which was ignited by the extreme Jihadist, turned the entire Europe in turmoil.</u>
Basic Question 53	The present interreligious conflicts in <u>France, which was ignited by the extreme Jihadist, turned the entire Europe in turmoil.</u> A) France, which was ignited by the extreme Jihadist, turned the entire Europe in turmoil. B) France, that ignited by the extreme Jihadist, turned the entire Europe in turmoil. C) France, which was ignited by the extreme Jihadist turned the entire Europe in turmoil. D) France ignited by the extreme Jihadist turned the entire Europe in turmoil.

SAT HACKERS RULE #53	**DOUBLE-COMMAS AS APPOSITIVE (PARENTHETICAL ELEMENTS)** An appositive is a noun or phrase that modifies the host noun right before it. It can be a word or a short combination of words. Ex) The heart of Europe, Paris, is invaded by another terrorism. The heart of Europe, Paris with more than 10% of Islam population, is invaded by another terrorism. The heart of Europe, Paris that has proclaimed the war against terrorism, is invaded by another terrorism. By putting two commas as parenthetical element, we mean a part of a sentence can be removed without changing the essential meaning of the sentence. Ex) Chad's dream, to become a national hockey player, is on the brink of fiasco. Lynn, his husband of the former Chairman in a big company, decided to buy an oil refinery company. Choice B is wrong because conjunction "that" cannot replace "which" in this sentence. Another error in B is the usage of active voice by eliminating "is" before ignited even though the sentence is followed by an agent "by", which requires the passive voice. Choice C is wrong because by omitting the second comma, the sentence lost the main verb, making an incomplete sentence. Choice D is wrong because the phrase "ignited by extreme Jihadist" is not an essential information. Therefore, that phrase requires double comma.
Harder Question 54	The actor Tom Cruise established his own film company.
Middle Question 54	The actor Tom Cruise established his own film company.
Basic Question 54	The actor Tom Cruise established his own film company. A) The actor Tom Cruise established B) The actor ,Tom Cruise, established C) The acting film star , Tom Cruise, established D) The actor as well as a film star Tom Cruise established

SAT HACKERS RULE #54	**OMITTING DOUBLE COMMAS** **If the appositive and the word it modifies are so closely related that double commas can be omitted.** **Tom Cruise is a well-known actor and we can regard "The actor Tom Cruise" as a one unit. In this case, if the double commas are used between "the actor" and "Tom Cruise", the sentence does not make any sense.** **Choice B is wrong because double comma should not be used.** **Choice C changes the meaning** **Choice D is wrong because it is wordy.**
Harder Question 55	**The doctor recommended his patient take three pills a day.**
Middle Question 55	**The doctor recommended <u>his patient take</u> three pills a day.**
Basic Question 55	**The doctor recommended <u>his patient take</u> three pills a day.** **A) his patient taking** **B) his patient take** **C) his patient takes** **D) that his patient to take**
SAT HACKERS RULE #55	IMPERATIVE VERB IN SUBJECTIVE MOOD The imperative verbs are used to give orders or instructions. When the imperative verb is used in subjunctive mood—that you desire or imagine something to be done or someone to do something, the model verb "should" can be removed and the base verb is used. Some typical imperative verbs are as follow: ask, demand, determine, insist, move, order, pray, prefer, recommend, regret, request, require, suggest, and wish. The subjunctive for the present tense third person singular drops the -s or -es so that it looks and sounds like the present tense for everything else.

SAT HACKERS RULE #55	Choice A is wrong because "taking" is gerund that can sound as a going concern. Choice C is wrong because in imperative verb like recommend already contains the meaning of "should". Therefore, the main verb should drop "s" or "es" and uses the base verb regardless of the subject. Choice D is wrong because that clause requires verb.
Harder Question 56	After I graduated high school, I have never been in a serious relation with anyone.
Middle Question 56	<u>After I graduated high school,</u> I have never been in a serious relation with anyone.
Basic Question 56	<u>After I graduated high school,</u> I have never been in a serious relation with anyone. A) NO ERROR B) With my graduation from high school C) Since I graduated high school D) When I graduated high school
SAT HACKERS RULE #56	SINCE AS THE PRESENT PERFECT TENSE "Since" always requires the present perfect tense in the main sentence. Therefore, the correct answer is C.
Harder Question 57	While reading a detective novel, my cat was sleeping inside my arms.
Middle Question 57	While reading a detective novel, <u>my cat was sleeping inside my arms</u>.
Basic Question 57	While reading a detective novel, <u>my cat was sleeping inside my arms</u>. A) my cat is sleeping inside my arms B) I held my sleeping cat inside my arms C) I fell asleep with my cat inside my arms D) a sleeping cat was inside my arms

Ch. 1

Ch. 2

Ch. 3

Ch. 4

Ch. 5

Ch. 6

Ch. 7

Ch. 8

Ch. 9

Ch. 10

SAT HACKERS RULE #57	**MODIFIER 1** Dangling Modifier: A descriptive phrase that begins a sentence with a comma after it must have noun or pronoun that it describes after the comma. Ex) Completely exhausted, the marathoner's uniform felt like wearing an armor. Completely exhausted, the marathoner in uniform felt as if he was wearing an armor. The correct answer is B.
Harder Question 58	Jenkins, the professor, invited his international students on Thanksgiving day to serve a traditional turkey, wearing an old pilgrim costumes.
Middle Question 58	Jenkins, the professor, <u>invited his international students on Thanksgiving day to serve a traditional turkey, wearing an old pilgrim costumes</u>
Basic Question 58	Jenkins, the professor, <u>invited his international students on Thanksgiving day to serve a traditional turkey, wearing an old pilgrim costumes.</u> A) on Thanksgiving day to serve a traditional turkey invited his international students, wearing an old pilgrim costumes. B) invited his international students on Thanksgiving day to serve a traditional turkey, which was wearing an old pilgrim costumes. C) invites his international students on Thanksgiving day to serve a traditional turkey, wearing an old pilgrim costumes. D) wearing an old pilgrim costumes, invited his international students on Thanksgiving day to serve a traditional turkey.

SAT HACKERS RULE #58	**MODIFIER 2** Misplaced Modifier : a descriptive phrase must be located immediately after or before the thing or person it supposes to describe. The correct answer is D as the modifier "wearing an old pilgrim costumes" must be located after the professor.
Harder Question 59	Whatever the majority of the board decides does not reflect the employees' pay increase.
Middle Question 59	Whatever the majority of the board <u>decides does not reflect the employees' pay increase.</u>
Basic Question 59	Whatever the majority of the board <u>decides does not reflect the employees' pay increase.</u> A) decides, reflect not the employees' pay increase. B) decides, does not reflect the employees' pay increase. C) makes on their decision do not reflect the employees' pay increase. D) decides does not reflect the employees' pay increase.
SAT HACKERS RULE #59	**THE USAGE OF DEPENDENT CLAUSE AS A SUBJECT** When an entire dependent clause is used as a sentence subject, it should be treated as a single noun. Whoever bought this house should be a very rich person. Other indefinite pronoun that uses singular verb everyone /everybody/everywhere/everything/someone /somebody/somewhere/ something/ anyone/anybody/anywhere/anything/no one/nobody/ nowhere/nothing/each (of these) /either (of these) /neither (of these) The correct answer is D.
Harder Question 60	For the past year, every effort by Republican senators to topple Obama care considering embarrassing failure.
Middle Question 60	For the past year, every effort by Republican senators to topple Obama <u>care considering embarrassing</u> failure.

Basic Question 60	For the past year, every effort by Republican senators to topple Obama <u>care considering embarrassing</u> failure. A) NO CHANGE B) care considered embarrassing C) care was considered embarrassingly D) care was considering embarrassingly
SAT HACKERS RULE #60	**SENTENCE FRAGMENTS** A sentence fragment does not have either subject or verb or both that does not function as an independent clause. The correct answer is C
Harder Question 61	Cancun was not my first destination for vacation, I found it too hot temperature there was unappealing at that time, even torturing myself going there, and respected the voice inside of me.
Middle Question 61	Cancun was not my first destination for <u>vacation, I found it too hot temperature there</u> was unappealing at that time, even torturing myself going there, and respected the voice inside of me.
Basic Question 61	Cancun was not my first destination for <u>vacation, I found it too hot there</u> was unappealing at that time, even torturing myself going there, and respected the voice inside of me. A) NO CHANGE B) vacation, because I found it too hot there C) vacation; because I found it too hot there D) vacation, but I found it too hot there

SAT HACKERS RULE #61	RUN-ON SENTENCES
	A run-on sentence contains multiple independent clauses without having a proper conjunction.
	Choice A is run-on, C is wrong for using semi-colon, D is wrong because wrong usage of conjunction but. The correct answer is B.
	Additional Example:
	Incorrect: If I were to leave for Hawaii now, on whatever the expenses, I could spend truly a lot more money on my vacation to expenses such as hotel, car rental, restaurant, the decision I finally made was Hawaii.
	Correct: But were I to leave for Hawaii now, on whatever the expenses, I could spend truly a lot more money on my vacation to expenses such as hotel, car rental, restaurant, so the decision I finally made was Hawaii.
	Incorrect: The worst-case scenario is that Hawaii in Christmas may be wholly unfit for the seasonal expectation, Hawaii is among the few which could expect no snow at all in winter.
	Correct: The worst-case scenario is that Hawaii in Christmas may be wholly unfit for the seasonal expectation because Hawaii is among the few which could expect no snow at all in winter.
Harder Question 62	The house that belongs to my tenant next to the backyard needs an additional repair.
Middle Question 62	The house that belongs to my tenant next to the backyard needs an additional repair.
Basic Question 62	The house that belongs to my tenant next to the backyard needs an additional repair. A) NO CHANGE B) The house that belong to my tenant C) The house of my tenant D) My tenant's house

SAT HACKERS RULE #62	POSSESSIVE SINGULAR NOUN A singular noun + apostrophe + s is the way to make a singular possessive noun The correct answer is D.
Harder Question 63	The recent data sent by Voyager II further confirms Dr. Ray's theory whom argued about water molecules in the Mar's atmosphere.
Middle Question 63	The recent data sent by Voyager II further confirms Dr. Ray's theory whom argued about water molecules in the Mar's atmosphere.
Basic Question 63	The recent data sent by Voyager II further confirms Dr. Ray's theory whom argued about water molecules in the Mar's atmosphere. A) further confirms Dr. Ray's theory, in which he B) further confirms Dr. Ray's theory, whom C) further confirms Dr. Ray's theory, by which he D) further confirms Dr. Ray's theory, who
SAT HACKERS RULE #63	WHO vs WHOM WHO is the subject pronoun, while WHOM is the object pronoun. The easiest way to find out the correct one is to look at the location of the verb. If there is a verb after the pronoun, "who" should be used. Meantime, If there is a subject and verb next to it, "whom" should be used. The correct answer is A
Harder Question 64	The passenger, who I saw yesterday, crippling and begging on the Mall, is standing right next to me, chatting with his friend.
Middle Question 64	The passenger, who I saw yesterday, crippling and begging on the Mall, is standing right next to me, chatting with his friend.
Basic Question 64	The passenger, who I saw yesterday, crippling and begging on the Mall, is standing right next to me, chatting with his friend. A) NO CHANGE B) The passenger that I saw yesterday C) The passenger, whom I saw yesterday D) The passenger, what I saw yesterday,

SAT HACKERS RULE #64	OBJECT PRONOUN WHOM. One trick to figure out whether "whom" is correct or not is to check if there is a subject follows after "whom". The correct answer is C.
Harder Question 65	The other side of the calculus that keeps the dark business humming is the crooked police. They are paid handsome sums of the profits.
Middle Question 65	The other side of the calculus that keeps the dark business <u>humming is the crooked police. They are paid handsome sums of the profits.</u>
Basic Question 65	The other side of the calculus that keeps the dark business <u>humming is the crooked police. They are paid handsome sums of the profits.</u> A) NO CHANGE B) humming is the crooked police, in which they are paid handsome sums of the profits. C) humming is the crooked police, who are paid handsome sums of the profits. D) humming is the crooked police, and they are paid handsome sums of the profits.
SAT HACKERS RULE #65	TWO SIMPLE SENTENCES INTO ONE As long as the person, place, or thing in two simple sentences are referring to each other, the best way is to combine them into one. The correct answer is C. Examples) Incorrect: After working together for 5 days, the five pushed a 100-pound steel beam down a steep tunnel. They crushed the woman to death. The five reported it to the police as an accident. Correct: After working together for 5 days, the five pushed a 100-pound steel beam down a steep tunnel, crushing the woman to death. The five reported it to the police as an accident.

SAT HACKERS RULE #65	TWO SIMPLE SENTENCES INTO ONE (Continued)
	Incorrect: Many farmers work in factories and on ramshackle building sites in that area. The area is now occupied by aging parents and grandparents.
	Correct: Many farmers work in factories and on ramshackle building sites in that area, which is now occupied by aging parents and grandparents.
Harder Question 66	American athletes win most medals in the Olympics whereby America has such great systems for preparing athletes.
Middle Question 66	American athletes win most medals in the Olympics <u>whereby America has such great systems</u> for preparing athletes.
Basic Question 66	American athletes win most medals in the Olympics <u>whereby America has such great systems</u> for preparing athletes. A) NO CHANGE B) because America has such great systems C) ;moreover, America has such great systems D) ;consequently, America has such great systems
SAT HACKERS RULE #66	CONJUNCTION FOR CAUSE-EFFECT CLAUSES Following conjunctions represent cause-and-effect relations between the clauses. -Because -Therefore -For example -Whereby -Consequently The correct answer is B.
Harder Question 67	In a war against the Islamic State, women can be found in the ranks but also in command of guerrilla units.

Middle Question 67	In a war against the Islamic State, <u>women can be found in the ranks</u> but also in command of guerrilla units.
Basic Question 67	In a war against the Islamic State, <u>women can be found in the ranks</u> but also in command of guerrilla units. A) NO CHANGE B) women can be found not only in the ranks C) women can be found by the ranks D) women can be found more in the ranks
SAT HACKERS RULE #67	CONJUNCTION FOR SIMILARITY Following conjunctions represent Similarity and emphasis -Moreover - just as - likewise - not only …but also The correct answer is B.
Harder Question 68	Some European industries have declined, and others are rising.
Middle Question 68	Some European industries have declined, <u>and others are rising.</u>
Basic Question 68	Some European industries have declined, <u>and others are rising.</u> A) NO CHANGE B) however, others are rising. C) since others are rising. D) but others are rising.

Ch. 1 Ch. 2 Ch. 3 Ch. 4 Ch. 5 Ch. 6 Ch. 7 Ch. 8 Ch. 9 **Ch. 10**

SAT HACKERS RULE #68	CONJUNCTION FOR CONTRADICTION
	Following conjunctions represent contradiction
	-However
	-on the other hand
	-but
	-nevertheless
	-aside from
	-while or whereas
	The correct answer is D.
Harder Question 69	The car making a squeaking noise as it veered to the right finally ran into the bakery.
Middle Question 69	The car <u>making a squeaking noise as it veered to the right</u> finally ran into the bakery.
Basic Question 69	The car <u>making a squeaking noise as it veered to the right</u> finally ran into the bakery.
	A) NO CHANGE
	B) made a squeaking noise as it veered to the right and
	C) which was making a squeaking noise as it veered to the right
	D) , making a squeaking noise as it veered to the right,
SAT HACKERS RULE #69	RESTRICTIVE MODIFIER
	If the clause requires a modifier to deliver the essential meaning, the modifier should not be surrounded by two commas.
	Choice B is MISUSED AND ERROR. C is out as it used unnecessary "Which was". The correct answer is A.

Harder Question 70	Some of the survivors in the refugee camps of Iraqi Kurdistan dominated by heavily patriarchal system shows how strong the tradition influenced the war.
Middle Question 70	Some of the survivors in the refugee camps of <u>Iraqi Kurdistan dominated by heavily patriarchal system shows</u> how strong the tradition influenced the war.
Basic Question 70	Some of the survivors in the refugee camps of <u>Iraqi Kurdistan dominated by heavily patriarchal system shows</u> how strong the tradition influenced the war. A) NO CHANGE B) Iraqi Kurdistan; dominated by heavily patriarchal system, shows C) Iraqi Kurdistan, dominated by heavily patriarchal system, show D) Iraqi Kurdistan, dominated by heavily patriarchal system show
SAT HACKERS RULE #70	NON-RESTRICTIVE MODIFIER If the modifier merely putting an additional information without losing the essential meaning, then the modifier should be surrounded by two commas. The correct answer is C

Made in the USA
Lexington, KY
15 December 2016